Artists in Profile

IMPRESSIONISTS

Jeremy Wallis

H **www.heinemann.co.uk/library**
Visit our website to find out more information about **Heinemann Library** books.

To order:
☎ Phone 44 (0) 1865 888066
▤ Send a fax to 44 (0) 1865 314091
▯ Visit the Heinemann Bookshop at www.heinemann.co.uk/library to browse our catalogue and order online.

First published in Great Britain by Heinemann Library, Halley Court, Jordan Hill, Oxford OX2 8EJ, a division of Reed Educational and Professional Publishing Ltd. Heinemann is a registered trademark of Reed Educational & Professional Publishing Limited.

OXFORD MELBOURNE AUCKLAND
JOHANNESBURG BLANTYRE GABORONE
IBADAN PORTSMOUTH NH (USA) CHICAGO

© Reed Educational and Professional Publishing Ltd 2002
Paperback first published in 2003
The moral right of the proprietor has been asserted.

Designed by Tinstar Design (www.tinstar.co.uk)
Originated by Ambassador Litho Ltd
Printed by South China Printing Company, Hong Kong/China

ISBN 0 431 11640 7   (hardback)
06 05 04 03
10 9 8 7 6 5 4 3 2

ISBN 0 431 11645 8   (paperback)
07 06 05 04 03
10 9 8 7 6 5 4 3 2 1

British Library Cataloguing in Publication Data
Wallis, Jeremy
   Impressionists. – (Artists in profile)
   1.Impressionism (Art) – Juvenile literature
   I.Title
   709'.0344

Acknowledgements
The Publishers would like to thank the following for permission to reproduce photographs:
AKG London p29; Bridgeman/Musee d'Orsay p20; Collection of the Butler Institute of American Art, Youngstown, Ohio p25; Corbis p24; Dreyfus Foundation, Kunstmuseum, Basel, Switzerland/Bridgeman Art Library p40; E. G. Buehrle Collection, Zurich/ AKG London p50; E. Lessing/Art Institute, Chicago/AKG London p7; E. Lessing/Musee des Beaux-Arts, Pau/AKG London p19; E. Lessing/Musee D'Orsay, Paris/AKG London pp5, 10, 12, 13, 17, 35, 36, 37, 45; Fitzwilliam Museum, University of Cambridge, UK/Bridgeman Art Library p51; Francis G. Mayer/Corbis p14; Hulton Archive p23; Illustrated London News Picture Library/Bridgeman Art Library p16; Musee D'Orsay/Bridgeman Art Library p53; Musee Marmottan, Paris/Bridgeman Art Library p9; National Gallery London, UK/Bridgeman Art Library pp22, 32; Nationalmuseum, Stockholm, Sweden/Bridgeman Art Library p47; Ny Carlsberg Glyptothek, Copehagen/AKG London p27; Philadelphia Museum of Art, USA/Bridgeman Art Library p15; Phillips Collection, Washington DC, USA/Bridgeman Art Library p48; Private Collection /Bridgeman Art Library p39; Private Collection/AKG London p8; Private Collection/Roger- Viollet, Paris/Bridgeman Art Library p31;Sheldon Memorial Art Gallery, F.M. Hall Collection p43.

Cover photograph: Les Alyscamps, by Vincent van Gogh. Superstock.

Our thanks to Richard Stemp for his help in the preparation of this book.

Every effort has been made to contact copyright holders of any material reproduced in this book. Any omissions will be rectified in subsequent printings if notice is given to the Publisher.

Contents

Words appearing in the text in bold, **like this**, are explained in the glossary.

What is Impressionism?

The Impressionists were a group of painters who changed the way artists look at the world and record what they see. Many – Cézanne, Degas, Manet, Monet, Pissarro, Renoir – are now household names. Others are less well known. Their work now commands fabulous prices, but little over a century and a quarter ago they were the vanguard of an artistic revolution.

Imagine a world where art schools tell artists how to paint, what to paint and where to paint. Where having a picture accepted for an art exhibition depends on the artist's willingness to abide by strict rules of picture composition, **perspective** and colour. Where only the great and the good – the rich or famous – have their portraits painted while ordinary people are considered unsuitable as subjects. Imagine a world that believes nature, in landscapes and seascapes, should be romanticized, prettified or entirely imagined by the artist. This was the situation in 19th-century France.

The Impressionists wanted to paint what they saw rather than what the rules said they ought to see. This idea of 'realist' art went against the 'idealization' wanted by the **art establishment**. Each Impressionist had their own ideas about art and differed in technique and subject. They often disagreed with each other. But they recognized that they had much in common and gathered together to exhibit their art.

The art establishment in France

For years France had had an elaborate system of teaching and exhibiting art. In Paris alone there were hundreds of art schools and **ateliers**. No other city had as many places to study art. It might be imagined that many artistic experiments took place, but this was not the case. The art establishment believed they knew the best, in fact the only way to paint. They controlled most of the art teaching and the major exhibition – the **Salon** – at which artists could make their reputation. They used their power to keep new artists in line; those who ignored the rules were often prevented from exhibiting.

The Salon

The official system of art teaching was crowned by the Salon – the annual exhibition of the Académie Royale de Peinture et Sculpture. The most important artistic event in the country, it made news around the world. Attendances were high. Pieces were chosen by a jury, which provoked bitter arguments because of the importance of being accepted. It was one reason the Impressionists banded together: they believed artists themselves should choose works they wanted to exhibit.

Most aspiring artists enrolled in the ateliers of established painters. One of the best known was that of Charles Gleyre. During his career Gleyre taught over 600 students, including Renoir, Bazille, Monet and Sisley. Gleyre was seen as eccentric because he valued originality. Bazille later said that thanks to Gleyre 'I shall at least be able to boast that I have not copied anybody.'

'Standing on the shoulders of giants'

Most artists spent time copying **Old Masters** to understand their techniques. Renoir said: 'It is in the museum that one must learn to paint.' Manet, Cassatt and Degas copied there. Only Monet was confident enough in his talent to believe he did not need to study these great works.

The Écoles des Beaux Arts

These were official art schools financed and run by the French government. At the top stood the École Nationale Supérieure des Beaux-Arts in Paris, founded in 1648. Many Impressionists attended, including Degas, Manet and Renoir. The conservative teaching methods increased their disappointment with the art establishment.

Le Bal au Moulin de la Galette (The Ball at Moulin de la Galette), by Auguste Renoir (1876)
Depicting a regular Sunday dance in Montmartre, Paris, this is one of Renoir's best-known paintings. He knew from his own experiences how hard the working lives of young Parisians often were and liked to show how they could also enjoy themselves.

Art in revolt

The Impressionists were revolutionary in several ways. Firstly, in their choice of subject. The **art establishment** believed people did not want to see reality but an idealized version of it. The public went along with this: they did not want realistic landscapes – they wanted to see perfect clouds, perfect trees, heavenly buildings. In portraits – the public wanted to see famous individuals, heroes, people of flawless beauty. They certainly did not want to hang pictures on their walls of people they would not allow into their homes!

However, realism attracted many painters, writers and poets. They were living in times of incredible scientific, social and industrial change and were often both fascinated and repelled by these changes. Industrialization altered the French landscape with railway bridges, tracks, factories and new towns. The Impressionists wanted to record these changes. Some Impressionists were interested in people, especially the new 'urban' classes – people who lived and worked in modern towns. They recorded the gaiety in people's lives – fêtes and dances, the circus, music hall and ballet. Others – notably the female Impressionists – also showed the sadness that affected people, especially women whose opportunities were limited by social rules.

The second way in which the Impressionists were radical was in how they painted. During the Renaissance (the explosion of art in 14th-century Italy) painters had adopted a certain viewpoint, or **perspective**, in their work. They established rigid scientific rules of perspective that were accepted for centuries. There were also fixed ideas about picture composition – how the subject should be positioned in the picture – and framing – what the frame or edge of the picture was allowed to cut off.

The Impressionists began to develop their own theories of perspective, colour and composition. From the mid-1800s new ideas arrived in France from abroad. A Universal Exhibition was held in Paris in 1855, a second in 1867 and a third in 1878 which exposed artists to artefacts from non-European cultures. They realized that rules they had been taught were not shared by other cultures. Paintings and prints from Japan were particularly influential.

The Impressionists loved Japanese art and were sometimes referred to as 'les Japonais' – 'the Japanese'. Degas adopted unconventional Japanese-style viewpoints and often bisected people in his pictures with the picture frame. Manet used Japanese-style colouring that simplified and flattened skin tones and reduced shadow. Monet began to eliminate detail to enhance the effect of the picture as a whole. Caillebotte foreshortened perspective and used unusual viewpoints.

Street in Paris, A Rainy Day, by Gustave Caillebotte (1877)
During the 19th century, Paris was reborn as a modern city. Streets were widened, boulevards and parks created. Cafés, concert halls and grand public buildings were opened. Life in this new metropolis fascinated many of the Impressionists. Caillebotte captured the extraordinary changes he and other Parisians witnessed.

One might imagine colour would be uncontroversial but even here there were rules. Artists painted on a dark base and painted shadows as black or dark brown even though observation told them the colours around shadows tinted them. Monet and Manet began to prime their canvases with a white base, which brightened the colours painted over them. Renoir and Pissarro used a bright **palette**, with Pissarro claiming to use only the primary colours – red, yellow and blue – mixing them to make 'secondary colours', such as orange, green and purple.

Artists were expected to paint in a studio and work in stages – preparatory sketches, detailed studies, the finished piece. Monet, Bazille, Renoir and Sisley recognized the value of painting outside – **en plein air** – where colours were more vivid. They said it was impossible to reproduce colours and shadows from preliminary sketches back in a studio. Newly developed paint tubes meant they could more easily use oil paints wherever they set their easels.

The development of the camera also helped. It captured a 'moment in time' and showed details of human and animal movement that had previously not been revealed. Photographs were also used as the starting point of compositions – for example, Monet's *Women in the Garden* was based on photographs from Frédéric Bazille's family album.

Impressionism also owes much to events in 1863: the **Salon** rejected work by hundreds of artists, including a painting by Manet called *Déjeuner sur l'Herbe*. The artists complained to the French Emperor Napoleon III and he ordered another exhibition to be held – of works refused by the Salon. It was titled the **Salon des Refusés**. Though Manet's painting grabbed the headlines, future Impressionists Pissarro and Cézanne also had work exhibited. The Salon des Refusés was important because it strengthened the commitment of radical artists and undermined the prestige of the official Salon. It also put Manet at the head of these radical tendencies.

Impressionists met to discuss ideas in many cafés but none was more important than the Café Guerbois, on Rue des Batignolles, Paris. Manet frequented the café and artists with studios nearby, such as Bazille, Caillebotte, Cézanne, Degas, Monet, Pissarro and Renoir, often came to meet him there. The Café Guerbois also attracted writers who did much to promote the new art, including Émile Zola and the poets Stéphane Mallarmé and Charles Baudelaire. Art critics called the painters who visited the Café Guerbois 'L'École des Batignolles' – 'the Batignolles School'. Several artists said they disliked the heated discussions about art but all admitted they had learned much.

The **Franco-Prussian War** of 1870–1 between France and Prussia resulted in a crushing defeat for France. An uprising by Parisian Republicans and workers unhappy with the new government – The Third Republic – followed the war. Known as the **Paris Commune**, it was suppressed with great brutality in May 1871. The war affected many artists. Monet and Pissarro left for London and several others served in the military. Bazille was killed. War and political rebellion created an atmosphere unfriendly towards 'artistic revolutionaries' and the public remained suspicious of the Impressionists for many years.

A girl with a basket of fruit, by Frederick Leighton (c.1862–3)
Imaginery figures based on ancient Greek and Roman myths were popular subjects for traditional artists whose work was accepted at the Salon.

Several female artists joined the Impressionists. They had to overcome additional obstacles in that social customs were against women becoming artists. Teachers and critics believed women were not intelligent enough to tackle many subjects. There was no state education in Fine Arts for women; the Écoles des Beaux-Arts did not admit women until 1897. Women also faced domestic pressure to marry and have families. Within Impressionism female artists were recognized for their abilities. They also occupied important organizational positions.

The Impressionist Exhibitions

Deciding not to submit work to the Salon, the Impressionists held their own series of eight exhibitions. The first one opened on 15 April 1874. The aim was to let artists choose their own work. The critic Louis Leroy wrote a derisive review entitled 'The Exhibition of the Impressionists' (after Monet's *Impression: Sunrise*), so giving the movement its name. The third exhibition, in 1877, was the first to be called an 'Impressionist' exhibition by the artists themselves.

The Impressionist period was very short – little more than 20 years – but it changed art for ever. All art that has followed it has been either a development from or a reaction to Impressionism.

Impression: Sunrise, by Claude Monet (1872)
It is believed that Monet took less than an hour to paint this picture which, more than any other, symbolized the Impressionist revolution.

Jean-Frédéric Bazille 1841–70

- Born on 6 December 1841 in Montpellier, Southern France.
- Died 28 November 1870 in Beaune-la-Rolande, Burgundy, France.

Key works

The Artist's Family on a Terrace near Montpellier, 1867–8
View of the Village, 1868
Studio in the Rue de la Condamine, 1870

Frédéric Bazille's tall figure dominates several paintings by fellow Impressionists. The writer Émile Zola described him as 'blond, tall and slim, very distinguished' and said he had 'all the noble qualities of youth: belief, loyalty, delicacy'. Pissarro called him 'one of the most gifted among us'.

The Artist's Family on a Terrace near Montpellier, by Frédéric Bazille (1867–8)
In 1867, the Salon rejected Bazille's first version of this painting. Bazille reworked it and his second version was accepted in 1868. Émile Zola praised its contemporary subject matter and 'love of truth'. Bazille portrayed himself on the far left of the picture.

Jean-Frédéric Bazille was born into a wealthy Protestant wine-growing family. He had several sisters. A family friend, the art collector Alfred Bruyas, stimulated the young man's interest in art. Bazille's family, however, wanted him to be a doctor. He began medical studies in Montpellier in 1859 but lacked interest and grew unhappy. In 1862 a compromise was reached: his family allowed him to divide his studies between medicine and art in Paris. He enrolled at the **atelier** of Charles Gleyre.

Bazille was an enthusiastic student. He met other students who shared his convictions – Sisley, Monet and Renoir. They began to paint outdoors (**en plein air**). Artists – even those who did preparatory sketches outside – were taught to complete work in a studio. Some believed a painting should reflect reality, which could only be achieved if it was completed outside. Such artists were criticized by the **art establishment**. In May 1863 Bazille and Monet went to the Fontainebleau Forest outside Paris. Bazille wrote: 'I have been with my friend Monet, who is quite good at landscapes; he has given me advice ... The forest is truly wonderful.'

Art took up Bazille's time and his medical studies suffered. In April 1864, after a painting trip to Honfleur, Normandy, with Monet, Bazille learned he had failed his medical exams. Supported by his parents, he decided to pursue a career in art. A generous allowance enabled Bazille to help friends: in 1865, for example, he invited Monet to share his studio. In 1866, Bazille submitted two canvases to the **Salon**. One was *Girl at a Piano*. 'I chose [a subject from] the modern period ... and that is what will get me rejected,' he said. Sure enough, Bazille's painting was rejected. (His second submission – an orthodox still life – was accepted.)

In January 1867, Bazille and Renoir rented a studio on the Rue Visconti. Monet joined them in September. That year, the Salon rejected Monet's *Women in the Garden*. Bazille bought it for 2500 Francs, paying 50 Francs a month.

In 1868, Bazille and Renoir settled near the Café Guerbois, a meeting place for radical artists. In 1869, the Salon accepted *View of the Village*, one of his best paintings. In 1870, *Summer Scene, Bathers* was shown. Success seemed to beckon: 'I am delighted ... Everyone ... talks about it.' Then, in July, France declared war on Prussia. Bazille joined the flamboyant *Zouaves*.

In November, during a skirmish at Beaune-la-Rolande, Burgundy, a Prussian sniper shot and killed Frédéric Bazille.

Gustave Caillebotte 1848–94

- Born 19 August 1848 in Paris.
- Died 21 February 1894 at Petit-Gennevilliers, near Paris.

Key works

Les Raboteurs de Parquet (The Floor Scrapers), 1875
Pont de l'Europe, 1876
Street in Paris, A Rainy Day, 1877
Self-Portrait, 1892

For years Gustave Caillebotte was 'the great unknown' of Impressionism. Only recently has the startling originality of his talent been recognized. Born in Paris in 1848, Caillebotte grew up in Petit-Gennevilliers, outside Paris. His father made a fortune supplying bedding to the French army. When he died in 1873, he left Gustave and his brothers Martial and René very well off. Gustave enrolled at the École des Beaux-Arts that same year.

Caillebotte had many interests. He studied engineering and boat-building before he took up art, was a keen oarsman, raced yachts and was an enthusiastic gardener.

Les Raboteurs de Parquet (The Floor Scrapers), by Gustave Caillebotte (1875)
Caillebotte's best-known works are superbly executed scenes of city life. He was one of the few painters to portray working men.

Caillebotte's boating knowledge brought him into contact with Monet, when he helped him build a boat studio. Renoir also shared Caillebotte's interest in boats: they often sailed on the River Seine together. (Renoir immortalized Caillebotte in *Le Déjeuner des Canotiers (The Luncheon of the Boating Party)* – see page 48.) Caillebotte also passed his enthusiasm for gardening to Monet: gardens later became Monet's principle **motif**.

Caillebotte showed several paintings at the Second Impressionist Exhibition in 1876. He continued to contribute to Impressionist exhibitions until 1882. He also helped organize them, using his diplomatic skills to soothe disagreements. Caillebotte's paintings recorded the rise of social groups that owed their existence to the development of the modern city. He was especially interested in the urban middle class. Caillebotte often used unusual viewpoints and was fascinated by dramatic **perspective**.

By the mid-1880s, Caillebotte was less involved with the exhibitions. One reason was the arguments that split the movement into factions. His painting style developed beyond Impressionism, and would inspire several **Neo-Impressionist** artists.

However, he remained friends with several Impressionists and supported them financially by paying high prices for their paintings. He gave money to buy Manet's *Olympia* for the nation in 1889. He also attended monthly 'Impressionist Dinners' between 1890 and 1894, where he and Renoir would argue ferociously. Renoir delighted in taunting Caillebotte, whose face turned red with anger. Despite these quarrels the two remained firm friends.

Caillebotte remained a bachelor all his life. He and his brother Martial were close, and shared a house in Petit-Gennevilliers until Martial got married in 1887. Caillebotte also shared this house with Charlotte Berthier. She is often described as his 'housekeeper'. Little is known about her though it seems likely she and Caillebotte were lovers. He left her the house and an income after his death.

Towards the end of his short life, Gustave Caillebotte stopped collecting pictures and exhibited little. He died on 21 February 1894, aged 45, of what was described as 'pulmonary congestion' – probably tuberculosis.

■ *Self-Portrait*, by Gustave Caillebotte (1892)
Painted two years before he died, this revealing self-portrait shows Caillebotte like a man haunted by a premonition of his own death.

Mary Cassatt 1844–1926

- Born 22 May 1844, in Allegheny City (now part of Pittsburgh), Pennsylvania, USA.
- Died 19 June 1926 near Paris, France.

Key works
Little Girl in a Blue Armchair, 1878
Woman and Child Driving, 1879
Mother about to Wash her Sleepy Child, 1880

Born in 1844, Mary Cassatt was the daughter of a wealthy banker, Robert Cassatt. Her mother Katherine was exceptionally well educated and spoke French fluently. Cassatt was very close to her sister Lydia. What made Cassatt an Impressionist was her interest in the everyday lives of modern women.

Mary Cassatt, Seated with Photographs, by Edgar Degas (1884) **Edgar Degas immortalised Cassatt in several paintings and etchings and was a major influence.**

Cassatt's interest in art was stimulated during a five-year family visit to Europe, between 1850 and 1855. As a teenager, she studied art privately and between 1861 and 1865 attended the Pennsylvania Academy of the Fine Arts. Though he had supported her while she studied, her father opposed her desire to be an artist, thinking it was not a suitable career for a woman. However, Cassatt was strong-willed and independent-minded – her father soon agreed. Cassatt returned to France in 1866. She enrolled in the **atelier** of Charles Chaplin, who organized women-only art classes. She also copied **Old Masters** in the Louvre. She had a painting accepted at the 1868 **Salon**.

At the outbreak of the **Franco-Prussian War** in 1870, Cassatt fled back to Pennsylvania. In 1872, she returned to Europe, visiting the museums of Italy, Spain and Holland before arriving in Paris in 1874. She grew unhappy with artistic orthodoxy but remained aloof from the Impressionists. However, the following year she saw work by Degas which, she claimed, changed her life. She continued to submit work to the Salon but her disenchantment grew when a picture rejected in 1875 was later accepted simply because she had darkened the background!

In 1877, after the Salon again rejected her work, a friend brought Degas to Cassatt's studio. They formed a friendship that was to last a long time. He invited her to join the Impressionists. 'I accepted with delight. I could work in complete independence, without ... the eventual judgement of a jury.'

That year, Cassatt's parents and her sister, Lydia, settled in Paris. Lydia became Cassatt's favourite model. Family life – especially the mother and child theme – became Cassatt's principal artistic **motif**. However, her pictures conveyed a melancholic loneliness that reflected the lack of opportunities then open to women. Lydia's death in 1882 upset Cassatt deeply. Cassatt exhibited with the Impressionists in 1879, 1880 and 1881. She also helped organize the final Impressionist show of 1886. Her work attracted excellent reviews.

Cassatt began to experiment with printmaking – making pictures from inked metal printing plates. In 1891, she exhibited Japanese-influenced prints and in 1893 created a mural for the Women's Building at the World Columbian Exhibition in Chicago. The theme was 'Modern Woman'.

Cassatt's father died in 1891, her mother four years later. Her inheritance enabled her to buy the Château de Beaufresne, near Paris. In 1898 she visited the USA for the first time in 20 years. In the 1900s, Cassatt's eyesight deteriorated. An operation to remove **cataracts** in 1911 was unsuccessful. By 1914 she had stopped painting. Instead she helped her friend Louisine Havermayer and her husband H. O. Havermayer to build their famous art collection.

Mary Cassatt died at Beaufresne on 19 June 1926. She never married – though rumours persisted about her relationship with Degas – and had no children.

Woman and Child Driving, by Mary Cassatt (1879)
Lydia Cassatt drives a carriage accompanied by Odile Fèvre, Degas' niece. What makes this interesting is the seriousness of the two people's expressions. The woman looks nervous while the child is lost in thought.

Paul Cézanne 1839–1906

- Born 19 January 1839 in Aix-en-Provence, France.
- Died 22 October 1906 in Aix-en-Provence.

Key works
Dr Gachet's House at Auvers, 1873
Portrait of Victor Chocquet, 1875–7
Still Life with Compotier, 1879–80

Though best known as a **Post-Impressionist**, Paul Cézanne made an important contribution to Impressionism during a short period of his career. He was the eldest child of Louis-Auguste Cézanne, a former hatter turned successful banker. He had two sisters, Marie and Rose. His mother Elizabeth Aubert was a full-time housewife, like most middle-class women of the time. Cézanne was a gentle but temperamental child. A good student at school, he excelled in maths, Latin and Greek. His earliest enthusiasms were writing and poetry. One of his school friends was the young Émile Zola. Cézanne often went on long walks with Zola in the countryside. He began to record these in drawings.

Mary Cassatt recalled meeting Cézanne, 'When I first saw him, he looked like a cut-throat ... I found later ... he has the gentlest nature.'

When he had completed his high school **baccalaureate**, Cézanne submitted to his father's wish and entered the family business. Cézanne studied law for three years, but painted in his spare time, copying **Old Masters** in Aix Museum. He tried to persuade his father to let him study art. In April 1861, after seeing paintings Cézanne had done to decorate the family home, his father relented.

Cézanne left for Paris but found the art scene hostile to new ideas and forever looking backwards. He was intimidated by the snobbery of his Parisian fellow students. Depressed, he stopped painting and returned home in the autumn. He took a job in his father's bank, but began painting again the following year. He returned to Paris in 1862 and enrolled at the Académie Suisse. It was here that fellow-student Camille Pissarro noticed the man's uncouth manners and provincial accent. Other fellow students made fun of these but Pissarro recognized and encouraged Cézanne's talent.

Cézanne frequented the Café Guerbois and met several artists who became leading Impressionists, including Manet and Renoir. He was infamous for his scruffy appearance and appalling manners. Throughout the 1860s Cézanne spent his winters in Paris and summers in Aix-en-Provence, painting all the time.

In 1870, he submitted two paintings to the **Salon**. He had done so before without success, and again his work was rejected. This time, however, he was ridiculed as an ignorant provençal in a newspaper. He responded that he would not compromise or produce pictures to please a Salon jury and declared he would paint as he felt and as he saw things.

Later that year he went to L'Estaque, near Marseilles, to escape military service in the **Franco-Prussian War**. He took his model, Hortense Fiquet, with him. The pair returned to Paris in late 1871 and in January 1872 they had a son, also named Paul. The family settled in nearby Auvers, and Pissarro began to direct Cézanne's powerful talent towards landscapes. Cézanne claimed Pissarro was like a father to him.

Cézanne exhibited with the Impressionists in 1874 and 1877, but critics were hostile and said they could not understand his art. By the late 1870s, Cézanne was bemoaning his lack of recognition compared to Renoir, Pissarro and Monet.

In April 1886, shortly before his father's death, Cézanne married Hortense. He alternated between Paris and Aix where he helped to care for his elderly mother. In 1895 an art dealer called Ambroise Vollard exhibited Cézanne's work. The exhibition was a success and Cézanne's reputation was established.

In 1906 Cézanne was caught in a rainstorm while painting. He collapsed by the roadside. He was later diagnosed with pneumonia, but insisted on going out to paint. His condition worsened and he died on 22 October 1906.

Dr Gachet's House at Auvers, by Paul Cézanne (1873)
This owes much to Pissarro's influence. Pissarro said of Cézanne:
'if ... he stays for some time at Auvers, he will astonish a lot of critics who were in too great haste to condemn him.'

Edgar Degas 1834–1917

- Born 19 July 1834, in Paris, France.
- Died 27 September 1917 in Paris.

Key works
Head of a Young Woman, 1867
The Cotton Exchange in New Orleans, 1873
Ballet Rehearsal, 1873–4
L'Absinthe, 1875–6
Miss La La at the Cirque Fernando, 1879

Edgar Degas was the son of a Parisian banker of Italian aristocratic birth called Auguste de Gas. The family owned a bank with branches in Paris and Naples, Italy. Degas' mother was a Creole of French descent born in New Orleans, USA. She married at sixteen, surrendered her life to bearing children and died after the birth of her seventh child when Edgar was thirteen. His was an affluent if melancholic childhood. Degas' father, an art collector, stimulated his son's interest in painting from an early age. Degas also saw paintings owned by family friends and was especially impressed by Ingres, the French artist. He began to draw members of his family. His father encouraged his son to develop his artistic talents.

Degas attended France's most prestigious boarding school – the Lycée Louis le Grand, Paris – from the age of eleven. It was a strict, austere school that prided itself on not teaching any arts subjects. He completed his **baccalaureate** in 1853 and, to comply with his father's wishes, studied law. He left his law studies after less than a year, determined to become an artist. After a family row he abandoned home and took a small attic lodging. Impressed, his father agreed to let Degas study art. Recognizing the strength of his son's determination and talent, he encouraged and supported him.

In 1853, Degas enrolled at the **atelier** of Louis Lamothe, a former student of Ingres. The year he spent there increased the respect he had for Ingres. Degas met him only once, and was advised: 'draw lines, young man, a great many lines'. Degas also enrolled at the École des Beaux-Arts that same year.

Degas was largely self-taught, however. He spent many months copying in the Louvre, and would return many times in the years to come. He abandoned formal studies in 1856 and travelled to Italy for three years. Availing himself of relatives' hospitality, he visited museums in Naples, Rome and Florence, copying great works, drawing relatives and discussing art with artists.

He returned to Paris in 1859 and moved into a studio on Rue Madame to continue his 'self-education'. Degas' main interests at that time were portraits and classically themed paintings but in 1862, in the Louvre, he met Édouard Manet. It was the beginning of a love-hate relationship. Manet persuaded Degas to take the modern world and the people around him as subjects.

Degas found favour with **Salon** juries and had work accepted by them from 1865. In 1869 *Portrait of Mme G.* was accepted – Berthe Morisot described it as 'a very pretty painting of a very ugly woman'. However, Degas grew hostile to the Salon juries' narrow, preconceived ideas of 'good' art.

During the **Franco-Prussian War**, Degas joined the National Guard, serving in Paris during the Prussian siege of 1871. He left after the city surrendered. In October 1872 Degas visited New Orleans. He enjoyed America but missed France: 'Everything is beautiful [here] but one Paris laundry girl with bare arms is worth it all for such a confirmed Parisian as I am,' he wrote to a friend.

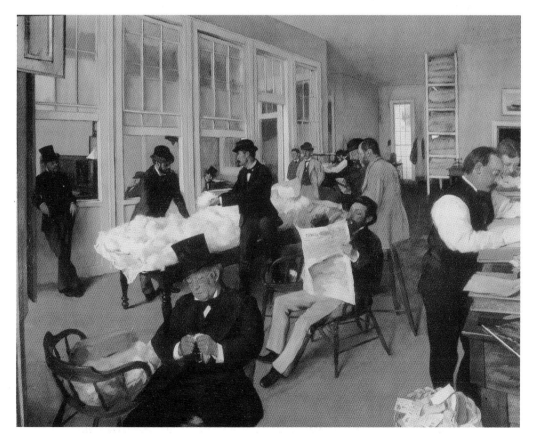

The Cotton Exchange in New Orleans, by Edgar Degas (1873)
Like a moment captured on camera, this painting encapsulates qualities Degas learned from Manet combined with his own unique artistic flair, producing social realism and a careful and sophisticated picture composition.

Degas had a proud, sarcastic and acerbic manner, but despite this his reputation grew. The writer Edmond de Goncourt described him as 'a bizarre painter – a strange fellow, neurotic, sickly, with bad eyesight – he's always frightened of going blind.' But he recognized that Degas was a great painter of the modern world: 'the most likely person I've met who can catch the spirit of modern life.' Degas visited music halls, concerts and circuses and attended the ballet three times a week. The performers' disciplined routines and ostentatious dress fascinated him: 'You need natural life,' he told contemporaries, 'I, artificial life.' (Half of Degas' total output would be on ballet themes.)

Degas submitted nothing to the **Salon** exhibitions after 1870 and criticized those who still presented works to them. He helped organize the 1874 Impressionist Exhibition as an independent alternative to the Salon.

Degas' father had died on business in Naples in 1873. In June 1876, soon after the second Impressionist Exhibition, Degas travelled to Naples to discuss the family firm's financial situation. This was not good – his brother René had been running the firm so badly it had incurred huge debts. In August, the intensely proud Degas assumed responsibility for these debts and sold his art collection

The Dance Foyer at the Opera on the Rue le Peletier, by Edgar Degas (1872)
The world of ballet would exert an enduring fascination for Degas and he completed many pictures, paintings and sculptures on this subject. By the end of his life one half of his total output would be on the ballet.

to avoid bankruptcy. Until now, Degas had not liked to part with his paintings, never believing they were 'finished', and he sometimes borrowed paintings back to work on them. It was rumoured collectors chained his pictures to their walls to stop him! However, his financial situation now made it important to sell work – much to his regret. By January 1877, Degas had made 20,000 francs, which he paid to the Bank of Antwerp.

At the third Impressionist Exhibition, in April 1877, there was a room devoted to Degas. Critics praised him. Though the Impressionists wanted to establish themselves as a coherent stylistic force, rivalries increased. Degas tried to stop it being called the *Exposition des Impressionistes*. He described himself as a 'realist' and liked to paint under artificial light, having completed many preparatory sketches and watercolours. He disliked painting **en plein air**, once remarking: 'the police should shoot down all those easels cluttering up the countryside.'

Despite the critics' approval, Degas' finances remained uncertain. Depressed, he wrote to a friend: 'To live alone without a family is too hard ... Here I am, getting old, and almost penniless. I have organized my life in this world very badly.' A mutual friend introduced Degas to Mary Cassatt in 1877. They became close. Rumours said they were lovers. Some believe Cassatt hoped to marry Degas, but he remained a bachelor all his life.

In 1878, an American friend of Cassatt, Louisine Waldron Elder, lent Degas' *Ballet Rehearsal* to the American Watercolour Society. It was the first Degas exhibited in the USA and was well received. The museum of Pau in Southern France bought *The Cotton Exchange in New Orleans*, so that it became his first work to go to a public collection. Degas' fortunes were improving. That year, Degas read about the American photographer Eadweard Muybridge who used cameras to capture animal and human movement. Degas called photography 'magical instantaneity'. He bought Muybridge's book of photographs *Animal Locomotion* and based several pictures of horses on them. (Degas later used photographs as the basis of paintings and as artworks in their own right.)

At the fourth Impressionist Exhibition, in April 1879, Degas showed 29 works. His influence was more powerfully felt in this exhibition: he insisted 'Impressionist' should not be prominent in the exhibition title and was able to include works of many protégés, including Cassatt. Labelled an exhibition by a 'Group of Independent Artists', it was a commercial success, but critics claimed the Impressionists were finished as a single, unified movement. 'You are invited to attend the funeral service ... of the Impressionists', one wrote.

Degas had a very difficult character. A journalist called him: 'aggressive, easily ... excited.' Paul Gauguin, beginning his own artistic career, witnessed Degas' attempts to force his own way: 'Degas ... has a perverse spirit which destroys everything.' Caillebotte, who described himself as 'a pupil of Degas', grew tired of Degas' stubbornness and bad temper. When Renoir, Sisley, Cézanne and Monet did not participate in the 1880 Exhibition because of Degas, Caillebotte accused him of introducing 'disunity into our midst'. However, Degas was excluded from the seventh Impressionist Exhibition in 1882 and the others returned.

Degas could be very kind. When the critic Edmond Duranty died, Degas arranged an art sale to help Duranty's mistress. He also played matchmaker for Julie Manet, orphaned daughter of Berthe Morisot.

Degas battled with deteriorating eyesight from 1870. Though he continued to work until five years before his death, it affected his style. Throughout his career he used paints, pastels and various printing techniques. As his eyesight worsened, he virtually abandoned painting and used pastels almost exclusively. By the 1890s he was also using photography – both to create images and to enable him to continue painting. Similarly, he had often sculpted and modelled during his career – a life-size wax sculpture *Little Dancer of 14 Years* (1879–81) was shown at the sixth Impressionist Exhibition – but when unable to use pastels, he turned exclusively to sculpture. He also wrote poetry.

Degas grew morose. In 1884, aged 50, he wrote: 'I always thought I had time; what I

Miss La La at the Cirque Fernando, by Edgar Degas (1879)
Degas visited the Cirque Fernando, a popular Parisian circus, which inspired several works. Miss La La ... *was one of the best-received paintings of the fourth Impressionist Exhibition.*

didn't do ... I never gave up hope of starting one fine day. I've hoarded all my plans in a cupboard of which I always carried the key, and I've lost that key.' He distanced himself from his contemporaries. He scolded Monet for submitting work to the **Salon** and accepting honours and praise. Gauguin wrote to Pissarro: 'Degas has greatly harmed our movement ... fortunately art has not suffered from this ... Degas is going to end his days more unhappy than the others.'

In 1886, Degas organized the eighth, and last, Impressionist Exhibition. Few original Impressionists participated. Degas shocked many with a series of nude women bathing. Meanwhile, the art dealer Durand-Ruel organized an Impressionist exhibition in New York. It contained 23 works by Degas, which were praised for their 'knowledge of life'.

■ *The elderly Edgar Degas. During World War I, as battles raged close to the city, he blindly wandered the streets of Paris. He had stubbornly refused to leave his beloved city when it was threatened in 1914.*

Degas encouraged new artists, including Gauguin, Georges Seurat and Paul Signac, but grew increasingly isolated. He no longer attended 'Impressionist Dinners' and lived a hermit's existence in Paris. His life was littered with ruined friendships: 'I quarrelled with all the world and with myself.' During the **Dreyfus Affair** of the 1890s, when an innocent Jewish army officer was jailed for passing secrets to Germany, Degas became vehemently **anti-Semitic**. Pissarro, who was Jewish, had stuck by Degas up till now but this was the final straw. In 1898, Degas returned to St Valéry-sur-Somme, where his parents had taken him as a child. Almost blind, he completed what would be his last landscapes.

Financially, Degas was very successful. His art collection included work by Ingres, Delacroix, Daumier, Manet, Pissarro, Cassatt, Morisot, Gauguin and van Gogh. However, at the end of his life he was isolated, unable to paint, surrounded by a collection of masterpieces he was too blind to enjoy. He died of a stroke at his Paris home on 27 September 1917. Renoir said: 'It is indeed the best for him ... Every imaginable kind of death would be better than to live as he was living.'

Childe Hassam 1859–1935

- Born 17 October 1859 in Dorchester, near Boston, USA.
- Died 27 August 1935 in East Hampton, New York, USA.

Key works
Rainy Day, Columbus Avenue, Boston, 1885
Manhattan's Misty Sunset, 1911
Fifth Avenue, April Morning 1917, 1917
Church at Gloucester, 1918

Frederick Childe Hassam was born in Dorchester, Massachusetts, USA in 1859. As a young man he began to use his second name, Childe, which was that of a favourite uncle, and sign his name F. Childe Hassam. He had literary relatives: his mother was a descendant of the novelist Nathaniel Hawthorne. His family ran a successful hardware business in nearby Boston. However, the business was destroyed in the great fire of 1872. With the family in financial straits, Hassam took a job in the accounts department of a Boston publisher, Little, Brown and Company.

In later years, Hassam became more conservative in his artistic outlook and in February 1913, he condemned the European avant-garde art on show at the International Exhibition of Modern Art at the New York Armory – known as the Armory Show.

Hassam had shown an interest and aptitude for art from an early age. His supervisor at work persuaded him to learn the craft of wood engraving. After his apprenticeship he became a freelance book and magazine illustrator. This enabled him to support himself while he studied art in evening classes at the Boston Art Club. He then studied at the Howell Institute before returning to the Boston Art Club in 1882. He began painting in and around Boston and during a trip to nearby Gloucester sold many watercolours. Encouraged, he committed himself to painting.

In 1883, Hassam made his first trip to Europe, stopping first in England, where he was impressed with the work of the English painter Joseph Turner. Sixty-seven watercolours from his trip were exhibited in Boston. Sales went well and a few months later he married Kathleen Maude Doane, whom he had courted for some time. They remained married for 50 years.

Many American artists travelled to Paris in the 1880s. The American writer Henry James commented: 'When today we look for 'American Art' we find it mainly in Paris. When we find it out of Paris, we at least find a good deal of Paris in it.' Hassam was no exception: he and his wife visited France in 1886. He was attracted to Impressionism and learned from it, making many rural and urban **plein air** paintings. He also wanted to refine his technique as an oil painter and studied at the Académie Julien in Paris. Like Degas, he was a strong believer in **draughtsmanship** and the importance of line.

The Hassams returned to the USA in 1889 and settled in New York City. Impressionism had become popular and Hassam's style put him in the centre of the emerging band of American Impressionists. He completed many landscapes of rural New England but is best known for his cityscapes of New York City.

In 1898, Hassam was one of several artists who claimed to be unhappy with the way the American National Academy of Design displayed paintings at their annual show and resigned to form their own group – 'The Ten'. In fact it was a ploy to draw public attention to their exhibitions. The Ten exhibited together for the next 20 years.

During World War I, Hassam produced many popular patriotic paintings. *Fifth Avenue, April Morning 1917* was seen as the ultimate development of his Impressionist style. In later years, Hassam rediscovered his interest in printmaking: 'I began my career in the graphic arts, and I am ending it in the graphic arts.' He died after a prolonged illness at home in New York, on 27 August 1935.

Manhattan's Misty Sunset, by Childe Hassam (1911)
Hassam is famous for cityscapes of New York. In this painting he used the skyline that visitors were calling 'the eighth wonder of the world' to create bold, abstract designs.

25

Édouard Manet 1832–83

- Born 23 January 1832, in Paris.
- Died 30 April 1883, in Paris.

Key works

The Spanish Guitar Player, 1861
Le Déjeuner sur L'Herbe, 1863
Olympia, 1863
The Execution of Emperor Maximilian, 1868–9
Le Bon Bock (A Good Glass of Beer), 1873
Bar at the Folies-Bergère, 1881–2

Édouard Manet was the son of a wealthy member of the judiciary, Auguste Manet. His mother was called Eugénie-Desirée. He attended the school of Abbé Poilup in Vaurigard and boarded at the Collège Rollin from the age of twelve. His father hoped he would study law but Manet was a poor scholar. (He had to stay at school for an extra year.) He did show a talent for drawing and at sixteen announced he wanted to be an artist. Horrified, his family promptly enrolled him as a naval cadet. However, his family's resistance crumbled after he had made a single voyage to Brazil, during which the boredom of 'nothing but sea and sky' was interspersed with seasickness. When Manet was asked to retouch the coloured rinds of the cargo of cheese they were carrying, the oil paints that he used led to an outbreak of lead poisoning in Brazil. In Rio de Janeiro, he caught **syphilis**, which would eventually kill him.

In 1850, Manet entered the **atelier** of Thomas Couture. He stayed for six years, but developed his technique copying works by the Spanish painters Velásquez and Goya in the Louvre. He also visited museums in the Netherlands, Germany, Austria and Italy. In the Netherlands, in 1851, Manet met Suzanne Leenhoff, a music teacher. They had a son, Léon, in 1852. Manet kept both a secret, fearing his father would disapprove of a lower-class woman and stop his allowance. (Manet married Suzanne in 1863, after his father's death.)

In 1861, the **Salon** accepted two of Manet's paintings. However, in 1863 they rejected *Le Déjeuner sur L'Herbe* and it became the centrepiece of the **Salon des Refusés**. To some, Manet's picture of a nude woman sitting between two men in modern dress was a triumph. To others it was pornography. Arguments also followed the Salon's acceptance of another nude, *Olympia*, in 1865. Nudes were only acceptable if they were depicted a long way away in time or place – in scenes from the ancient world or of 'primitive people'. Manet interpreted classical ideas to put nudity into the 'here and now'. (He based the subject of *Olympia* on a painting by Titian, updating it so she resembled a prostitute.)

Many young artists, including Bazille, Monet, Degas, Renoir, Pissarro and Cézanne, congregated around Manet in the Café Guerbois. He was charismatic, funny and attractive. In the left-wing newspaper, *L'Evènement*, the writer Émile Zola praised Manet as 'a man of great sensitivity and kindness'. Manet had great influence. At the 1868 Salon, critics said Renoir's *Lise with a Parasol* was a Manet imitation. Many believed Manet had radical views. The art historian Bernard Denvir describes him as 'an upper-class Republican', who wanted to replace the empire with a republic. But Manet enjoyed the privileges of his class and sought official recognition. He wrote: 'Monsieur Manet has ... no intention of overthrowing old methods of painting.'

■■■ *The Execution of Emperor Maximilian*, by Édouard Manet (1868–9)
This is often cited as evidence of Manet's republicanism. In 1863, France invaded Mexico and made Maximilian, the brother of the Austrian ruler, Emperor of Mexico. When the Mexicans revolted, the French abandoned Maximilian and he was executed. Manet, like others, blamed the French Emperor Napoleon III for the fiasco. Emphasizing his point, the firing squad are pictured in French uniform.

He never exhibited with the Impressionists and used his portrait skills to flatter influential people. Degas said: '[Manet] felt only one ambition, to become famous and earn money.'

In 1869 Manet tackled the problem occupying his friends – how to capture a single moment on a quickly painted canvas. He spent the summer in Boulogne on the French coast and completed several works that captured events as they happened. 'One does not paint a landscape, a seascape, a figure,' he later said, 'one paints the impression of an hour of the day.' Manet had a fierce temper. In 1870, he fought a duel with a friend, art critic Edmond Duranty. 'Completely ignorant of ... fencing, Manet and Duranty threw themselves upon each other with such savage bravery ... their swords appeared to have been turned into ... corkscrews,' a witness reported. Duranty was slightly injured but both were friends again within hours! Manet and Degas often argued. Degas said Manet never did a brushstroke 'without the masters in mind'. Manet never let Degas forget it was he who encouraged Degas to portray modern life. When the **Franco-Prussian War** broke out in 1870, Manet sent Suzanne and Léon to Oloron-Sainte-Marie in the Pyrenees. During the **Siege of Paris** he joined the National Guard. He visited Berthe Morisot's home with his brother, Eugène. Manet enjoyed the war and, Morisot wrote, 'spent ... the siege changing uniform'. Manet asked the artist Eva Gonzalès to paint him in uniform.

Eva Gonzalès

Eva Gonzalès was born into an aristocratic Monaco family on 5 May 1849. She produced many works: 85 were shown at a **retrospective** in 1885. In 1867, she enrolled at the **atelier** of Charles Chaplin in Paris. In 1869 she met Manet, who asked her to model. She agreed to do this in exchange for art lessons, to her father's consternation because he did not think a career in art was appropriate for a woman.

Gonzalès submitted The Little Soldier (1870), based on a painting by Manet, to the 1870 **Salon**. She spent the Franco-Prussian War in Dieppe. She stayed inside the official system and continued to submit pieces to the Salon – though they were often rejected. She did not participate in the Impressionist exhibitions. Her models were often drawn from her immediate circle, especially her sister Jeanne and husband Henri Guérard.

In 1883, five days after the birth of her first child, Eva Gonzalès died of an obstruction of a blood vessel. She was 34 years old.

He reported the hardships to Suzanne. In September he wrote: 'We eat meat only once a day.' In November: 'Marie's big cat has been killed, and we suspect somebody in the house; it was for a meal, of course, and Marie was in tears!' Manet left for the Pyrenees after Paris surrendered in January 1871. He returned in time to see the suppression of the **Paris Commune** by the government. He demonstrated his sympathy for the Communards in a series of etchings.

Manet's fortunes improved after the war. He sold work to the art dealer Paul Durand-Ruel. His painting *Le Bon Bock* was well received at the 1873 Salon. Believing the **art establishment** was ready to accept him, he did not take part in the 1874 Impressionist exhibition. However, in 1876 two submissions to the Salon were rejected. Manet organized shows at his studio. He had 4000 visitors to these, which confirmed his celebrity status.

In 1877 Manet developed the first symptoms of locomotor ataxia, a crippling illness associated with **syphilis**. In 1881 Manet received a Second-Class Medal from the Salon and was appointed *Chevalier de la Légion d'Honneur* (Knight of the Legion of Honour). He complained it had arrived too late. By 1883, Manet was desperately ill. He developed gangrene in his left leg and it was amputated on 19 April. Fame made his illness a public event. Daily bulletins were posted outside his home. He died at Rueil, near Paris, on 30 April, aged 51 years.

▮▮▮ *Édouard Manet was the most notorious artist of his day. Because his subjects – nudes in modern settings; pictures with republican sympathies; informal portraits – outraged the artistic establishment, he became a hero to younger artists and had a huge impact on Impressionism.*

Claude Monet 1840–1926

- Born in Paris on 14 November 1840.
- Died Giverny, Normandy, France on 5 December 1926.

Key works

Déjeuner sur l'Herbe, 1865
Camille: Woman in the Green Dress, 1866
The Thames and the Houses of Parliament, 1871
Impression: Sunrise, 1872–3
Haystacks, 1890–1
The West Front of Rouen Cathedral, 1892
The Nymphéas (Waterlilies), 1916–26

Claude Monet is the best-known Impressionist. He was born in Paris in 1840 and his family moved to Le Havre when he was five. His father was a wholesale grocer and ships' chandler (a supplier of equipment for boats). His parents and teachers thought Claude undisciplined. 'It seemed like a prison,' he later said of school, 'and I could never bear to stay there.' Art was his only interest, and he earned a reputation for doing caricatures (cartoon portraits) of teachers. He earned money drawing caricatures of tourists on local beaches.

Monet left school at fifteen. He was soon earning more than his teachers doing caricatures to order. In 1858 he met a local artist, Eugène Boudin, who recognized the young man's talents and steered him towards painting – especially landscapes and open-air painting. Monet later claimed Boudin 'tore the veil from my eyes'. Monet and his father had a difficult relationship. Monet maintained his father wanted to crush his artistic ambitions. In fact, his father encouraged them, believing they would instil discipline into his son. He let Monet study in Paris. In 1859 Monet enrolled at a lackadaisical **atelier** and wasted much of his time.

Monet's father believed he could put a stop not to his son's artistic ambitions but to his unruly ways. Like many young men of those times, Monet was liable for military service. Wealthy parents often paid a substitute to serve in their son's place, but Monet's father refused to help unless he abandoned his carefree lifestyle. Monet greeted this 'with a superb gesture of indifference' and signed up for seven years!

Monet joined a regiment in French Algeria in 1860. He came home two years later with typhoid. Warned a return to the army might kill him, Monet's father bought him out. Monet's aunt then offered to help if he agreed to undertake a proper art course. Monet agreed. In November 1862 he joined the Paris atelier of Charles Gleyre. He befriended fellow students Renoir, Sisley and Bazille. Rebellious by nature and certain of his ideas, Monet became their leader. Though he disliked the idea of being 'taught', he stayed for eighteen months, until Gleyre's studio went bankrupt. (Monet claimed he studied there for only a week and refused to acknowledge Gleyre's teaching.) Monet's stubbornness continued to frustrate his family in Le Havre – his allowance was often cut.

In 1863, Monet and Bazille travelled to the Fontainebleau Forest to paint **en plein air**. Monet believed paintings – even portraits – could only be created realistically in natural light. In 1865, Monet made his first submissions to the **Salon** – two seascapes. A critic wrote of one of them: 'Monet, unknown yesterday, has ... made a reputation by this picture alone.' (Monet's paintings were hung near Manet's, who was praised for them in error: 'I am being complemented only on a painting that is not by me.') In 1866 Monet exhibited *Camille: Woman in the Green Dress* based on his model and mistress, Camille Doncieux, whom he met in 1863. The writer Émile Zola praised him, and Monet's family, pleased with the attention, resumed paying his allowance.

Claude Monet pictured in front of the *Nymphéas* (Waterlilies). *In old age, Monet dedicated himself to completing this last, great series of paintings as a celebration of the glory of France.*

Money was a persistent worry for Monet. His allowance was irregular, his outgoings on rent, materials and food were considerable and he was not selling work. In 1866, Monet fled to Ville-d'Avray, in the Ile de France, to escape creditors (people to whom he owed money). Late that year, Camille became pregnant. In July 1867 Monet revealed her condition to his family, hoping for their sympathy. Monet's father invited him to come home – and leave Camille in Paris. Desperate, Monet went to Le Havre. He could not even raise the train fare to be with Camille when she gave birth to their son, Jean. Monet finally returned to Paris in the autumn to be with Camille and Jean. He joined Bazille and Renoir at their studio.

The year 1868 did not start well. Monet and Camille were so poor they could not buy coal: 'My painting doesn't go ... I see everything black ... money is always lacking.' The family stayed on the Normandy coast. 'I spend my time

■■■ *La Grenouillère*, by Claude Monet (1869)
Working without preparatory stages, the paintings quickly produced at La Grenouillère by both Monet and Renoir perfectly captured the sparkle of the water, the light in the trees, the bright reflections of the day-trippers' clothes.

out of doors,' he wrote to Bazille. 'On the pebble beach ... or I go into the country ... And then in the evening, my dear friend, I find a good fire and a cosy little family in my cottage.' Submissions to the **Salon** were rejected. Artistically, Monet's breakthrough came in 1869 when he and Renoir painted at La Grenouillère ('the frogpond'), a restaurant and bathing place on the River Seine.

Monet spent summer 1870 painting in Le Havre and the resort of Trouville. In June he and Camille married. Still a member of the military reserve and likely to be called up, Monet fled to London at the outbreak of the **Franco–Prussian War**. Camille and Jean stayed behind, in the care of Boudin. Monet spent time with Pissarro in London and met the art dealer Paul Durand-Ruel, also a refugee, and persuaded him to take his paintings. Monet produced many paintings while in London and often returned in later years. He went back to France after the fall of the **Paris Commune** and settled in Argenteuil with Camille. His fame, if not fortune, was increasing. Friends helped, but his newest patron was an ostentatious businessman, Ernest Hoschedé.

In 1873, still frustrated by his lack of recognition, Monet returned to an idea he had discussed with Bazille years before, of a group exhibition. By 1874, the dream was a reality, and exhibitors were invited to show what they liked. At this first exhibition, Monet's painting *Impression: Sunrise* gave the whole Impressionist movement its name.

In 1876, Monet and Hoschedé's wife Alice formed a close relationship. Two years later, Hoschedé lost his fortune. He sold his Impressionist paintings at a disastrous auction that made little money. Alice and her six children joined the Monets in their house in Argenteuil. Ernest moved to Paris, to pursue what he called 'an impoverished bachelor life'. Camille gave birth to a second son, Michel, in 1878. She never recovered from the birth and by 1879 was very sick.

Marie Bracquemond

Marie Quiveron Bracquemond was born in 1841. As a young woman she studied under the great French painter Ingres. In 1869 she married Félix Bracquemond, an etcher and printmaker. He introduced her to the Impressionists. Of Monet she said: 'He opens my eyes and makes me see better.' Bracquemond began to depict contemporary life, and exhibited with the Impressionists in 1879, 1880 and 1886.

Félix grew jealous of her talent and rarely showed her work to visitors. Pierre, their son, recorded her difficulties. Bracquemond abandoned painting around 1890. She continued to support Impressionist principles until her death in 1916 at Sèvres.

Monet pawned their possessions to pay for medical care. He wrote to a friend: 'Please ... retrieve from the pawnshop the locket ... It is the only memento that my wife has been able to keep and I should like to tie it around her neck before she leaves forever.' Camille died on 5 September 1879. As she lay dying, Claude captured on canvas death's final onslaught: 'I caught myself ... searching for the ... coloured gradations [changes in colour] that death was imposing on her motionless face.' Monet later compared the experience of seeing everything purely in terms of art to that of an animal harnessed to a millstone.

In 1880, Monet agreed, under pressure from an art dealer, to exhibit at the **Salon** – to the fury of Pissarro and Degas. He also began to hold one-man shows, encouraged by Durand-Ruel. These were more successful and actually made money. By 1882, Monet was earning good money through Durand-Ruel. (Monet contributed to one more Impressionist exhibition, in 1882, and submitted nothing to the Salon after 1880. Quite simply, he did not need them any more.)

Monet's domestic situation was also more settled. In 1881, he, Alice and their respective children moved to a house at Poissy. (They eventually married in 1891, after Ernest Hoschedé's death.) In 1883, the family moved to Giverny, which remained Monet's home until his death.

Financial security led Monet towards the production of paintings in series – sets of pictures using the same subject, that differed according to the time of day, environmental conditions or season. He began his series paintings – rather haphazardly – in the 1870s with a sequence of views of Westminster Bridge in the fog in London and the steam-enshrouded Gare Saint-Lazare railway station in Paris. 'Serialism' became one of his most original contributions to art: an attempt to show the passage of time on a single subject. In 1891 he exhibited fifteen canvases of haystacks. He completed sequences of the *Valley of the Creuse* (1889), *Poplar Trees on the Epte River* (1891), *The West Front of Rouen Cathedral* (1892) and *The River Thames* (1899–1903). Julie Manet, the fourteen-year old daughter of Berthe Morisot, recalled a visit to Giverny in 1893: 'Monsieur Monet showed us his 'cathedrals'. There are twenty-six ... These pictures ... are an admirable lesson in painting.' Serialism brought its own problems, however. In May 1889, Monet wrote to Alice complaining he had to employ workmen to remove the leaves from an oak tree in order to finish a winter landscape!

In 1911, Alice died. Monet, now over 70, was cared for by one of Alice's daughters who had married Monet's eldest son Jean. In 1914, Jean died. Monet was deeply affected by both deaths.

Two events provided the motivation for Monet's great series *The Nymphéas (Waterlilies)*. In 1912, it was discovered Monet had **cataracts**. His eyesight deteriorated and *The Nymphéas* were partly a response to the problems he had distinguishing colours. World War I also gave Monet an incentive: he believed a monumental work would pay tribute to France and establish his reputation. Commissioned by Prime Minister Georges Clemenceau, twelve huge panels recorded the changing reflections on Monet's lily-ponds. In 1921, it was decided they would be hung in the Musée de l'Orangerie, Paris. In 1923, an operation on his cataracts allowed Monet to continue working. He worked on the *Nymphéas* until his death, on 5 December 1926, at the age of 86.

The Nymphéas (Waterlilies), by Claude Monet (1916–26)
Monet created a water garden at Giverny and it was here he painted his last, and many believe greatest, series: The Nymphéas (Waterlilies).

Berthe Morisot 1841–95

- Born 14 January 1841, Bourges, Central France.
- Died 2 March 1895, Paris.

Key works
The Mother and Sister of the Artist, 1870
The Cradle, 1872
Young Woman in a Ball Gown, 1876
Eugène Manet and his Daughter at Bourgival, 1881

Berthe Morisot holding a bunch of Violets, by Édouard Manet (1872) *Though the Impressionists were much more tolerant of women artists, Morisot is sometimes better known as a model than as an artist in her own right.*

Berthe Morisot was the third daughter of Edmé-Tiburce Morisot, the Prefect (government official in charge of towns and cities in France) of Bourges. The 18th-century painter Jean-Honoré Fragonard was a distant relative on her mother's side. Little is known about her childhood, except that she grew up in a cultured environment, and liked reading, playing the piano and clay modelling. The family travelled wherever her father's job took him, but in 1855 they settled in Passy, a suburb of Paris near the wooded Bois de Boulogne. Though she often travelled, Berthe lived in Passy for the rest of her life. Her work often featured the Bois de Boulogne.

In 1857, when Berthe was sixteen, her mother paid for her and her two sisters, Edma and Yves, to take art lessons. Yves lost interest but Berthe and Edma continued. As women they were barred from the École des Beaux-Arts so took lessons from Joseph-Benoît Guichard. Berthe and Edma decided they wanted to paint **en plein air**. Guichard recommended that they study under the artist Corot, who gave them lessons between 1861 and 1862. Both sisters submitted work to the **Salon** in 1864, which was accepted. In 1867, Berthe exhibited at a Paris gallery and had two paintings accepted at that year's Salon.

Morisot often copied the **Old Masters** in the Louvre, where she noticed Édouard Manet. Soon after, Manet and Morisot were formally introduced, either by Henri Fantin-Latour or Edma's fiancé, Adolphe Pontillon. (Pontillon served with Manet during the latter's time as a naval cadet.) Morisot was influenced by Manet's technique and emphasis on design. She encouraged him to experiment with outdoor painting. She also posed for him. Morisot's male colleagues often tried to 'improve' her work. Once Manet repainted her picture *The Mother and Sister of the Artist* (1870). She was furious! Her best pieces were intimate portraits of domestic life. They often featured Edma. By 1874, Morisot had developed her own unique style.

Morisot remained in Paris during the Prussian siege. The hardships and severe food shortages affected her health in later life. Degas, Manet and Manet's brother Eugène were regular callers at her home. Of Degas, Morisot wrote that he was: 'a little mad, but charmingly witty'. She married Eugène Manet in 1874. He tirelessly promoted his wife's talent.

Morisot's interest in outdoor painting and the dramas of everyday life propelled her towards Impressionism. She was the only woman to take part in the 1874 Exhibition and showed work at seven of the eight Impressionist Exhibitions, only missing the 1879 show after the birth of her daughter. Morisot exerted an influence she would never have enjoyed at the Salon. Her home became a social centre for the Impressionists. Her daughter, Julie Manet, became her favourite model. She charted Julie's growth for fifteen years.

By 1880, Morisot was at the height of her powers. Fellow Impressionists admired her work and Degas was one of her keenest supporters. Eugène Manet died in April 1892. In March 1895, Morisot developed pneumonia. She wrote: 'My little Julie, I love you ... I shall go on loving you after I am dead; please don't cry for me ...' She died on 2 March 1895, aged 54. After her death Degas arranged a memorial exhibition and also helped bring Julie together with the son of a friend. Despite her reputation, Morisot's death certificate records her as 'sans profession' – 'without profession'. Her position as an artist was not officially recognized.

The Cradle, by Berthe Morisot (1872)
In this portrait of Edma and her baby daughter, Berthe managed to capture an air of sadness. Edma had been successful at the Salon but found it difficult to paint after her marriage.

Camille Pissarro 1830–1903

- Born Saint Thomas, Danish West Indies, Caribbean, 10 July 1830.
- Died 13 November 1903, Paris.

Key works

Lower Norwood, London: Snow Effect, 1870
Lordship Lane Station, Dulwich, 1871
The Red Roofs: Corner of the Village, Winter Effect, 1877
Portrait of Félix Pissarro, 1881
The Gleaners, 1889
The Rooftops of Old Rouen, Grey Weather, 1896
The Place du Théâtre Français, 1898

Camille Pissarro was born on Saint Thomas, an island in the Caribbean. His father's family originated from Portugal. They were Marranos – Jews forcibly converted to Christianity by the Catholic organization called the **Inquisition**. The family later reconverted to Judaism. Pissarro's father Frédéric travelled from Bordeaux, South West France, to Saint Thomas in 1824, to carry out his late uncle's will. He fell in love with his uncle's widow, Rachel, who came from the Dominican Islands. When she fell pregnant, they announced their intention to marry. The Synagogue (Jewish temple) refused to acknowledge the wedding, and they were forced to marry away from the synagogue in 1825.

According to the art historian Joachim Pissarro (great-grandson of Camille Pissarro), Camille and his three siblings were deemed illegitimate and they attended an all-black primary school run by a Protestant body – the Moravian Brethren – instead of the white school. However, in 1833 the Synagogue recognized the marriage and therefore the legitimacy of the children, when Camille was three. There may be other reasons why Frédéric sent Camille to the Moravian school – such as the fact that his older siblings were already there or Frédéric's own wilfulness. (When he died, Frédéric willed his money equally between the Protestant Church and the Jewish Synagogue.)

The Pissarros ran a haberdashery store in the port of Charlotte Amalie. Many merchant ships called every week and Saint Thomas became a major trade centre between the Americas, Europe and Africa. As a boy, Camille spoke French at home and English and Spanish with the black population of the island. He began to draw – often portraying the black people he saw around him, of whom many were still slaves. He would often revisit the theme of people at work.

Anxious that his son should have a good – that is, French – education, Frédéric sent Camille to boarding school in France in 1842. His teachers, recognizing the child's artistic ability, encouraged him to sketch whatever he saw. Camille returned to Saint Thomas in 1847 to join the family business, but instead of supervising cargoes he sketched the vibrant harbour life, to his father's exasperation. In 1852, unable to persuade his father to let him study art, Pissarro ran off to Venezuela with a Danish artist, Fritz Melbye: 'Living in Saint Thomas ... I could not endure the situation any longer ... I abandoned all I had there and fled.' He worked in Caracas as an artist for two years.

Finally reconciled to his son's ambition, Frédéric insisted he should study in Paris. Pissarro returned to the French capital in 1855. He met Armand Guillaumin and Paul Cézanne at the Académie Suisse. He also encountered likeminded artists at the Café Guerbois. According to art historian John Rewald, Pissarro became 'a welcome guest ... for there was no one ... who did not feel a deep esteem for this gentle and calm man ... the most distrustful, most undependable members of the group, Cézanne and Degas, felt real friendship for him.'

Soon after he arrived in Paris, Pissarro's parents left their business with a caretaker manager and settled in the French capital. They hired a maid from Burgundy, called Julie Vellay. In 1860, Pissarro and Julie began a relationship. Their first child – Lucien – was born in 1863. Though they married in London, in 1871, Vellay's low social origins stopped her participating in Pissarro's social life.

When Pissarro's father died in 1865, Pissarro's allowance ended. He was forced to do odd jobs, including painting decorative window blinds with Guillaumin. In 1869, Pissarro and his family moved to Louveciennes. The following year, they fled to London before the Prussian advance, leaving almost all Pissarro's work behind. Prussian troops billeted in his house used the artworks as floor coverings. Of 1500 works, only 50 survived.

■■ *Throughout his life Pissarro was interested in the daily lives of working people and was the most politically active and left wing of the Impressionists. Some ascribe this to his childhood experiences in the Danish West Indies where he witnessed the effects of slavery at first hand.*

The Pissarros returned to Paris in June 1871. Camille became an energetic member of the Impressionists and the only one to participate in all their exhibitions. In 1872, the Pissarros moved to Pontoise. Financial problems continued and in late 1874 the family had to lodge with a friend. In 1878 Pissarro wrote: 'I am going through a frightful crisis.' He owed money and Julie was pregnant with their fourth child.

Pissarro always nurtured new talent. Many turned to 'Père (Father) Pissarro' for advice. He was an inspiring teacher. He never pressed his beliefs: 'Scorn my judgement. I cannot hide my opinions from you. Accept only those that accord with your sentiments.' He also had a warning: 'After thirty years of painting ... I am [still without money]. Let the younger generation remember!'

The Gleaners, by Camille Pissarro (1889)
Pissarro tackled many subjects: landscapes, native figures, cityscapes, river scenes, gardens, winter scenes. The Gleaners was painted in Éragny-sur-Epte, where the Pissarro family settled in 1884.

Pissarro was an adventurous artist. During the 1880s, he adopted **Pointillism**. At the last Impressionist Exhibition, in 1886, his work was hung alongside that of the **Neo-Impressionists**. He abandoned Neo-Impressionism during the 1890s and re-adopted Impressionism. Some accused him of copying others, but the artist Gauguin retorted in 1895: 'He looked at everybody, you say! Why not? Everyone looked at him, too, but denied him. He was one of my masters and I do not deny him!'

Pissarro's reputation grew more slowly than that of contemporaries and his family often lived in near-poverty. Only his commitment to his art kept his morale high. He was intensely proud of his family. 'Such is this family,' he wrote, 'where art is in the home, where each one of them, young and old, cultivates the rarest flowers of beauty.' Sadly, in 1897, as Pissarro was finally recognized as a great artist, his eldest son Lucien (who had also become an artist) had a stroke. In November that year, his third son Félix died of tuberculosis, aged 23.

The year 1897 saw the **Dreyfus Affair** divide France. Though Pissarro admired Degas, he found his **anti-Semitism** intolerable and ended their friendship. Pissarro suffered eye trouble and underwent several operations. Nevertheless, he painted until the end of his life. Years before he had written: 'What I am suffering now is terrible ... Yet I think that if I had to start all over again, I would not hesitate to follow the same path.' Camille Pissarro died in Paris on 13 November 1903, aged 73.

Armand Guillaumin (1841–1927)

Born in Paris on 16 February 1841, Armand Guillaumin lived in Moulins until he was fifteen, when he was sent back to Paris to work for his uncle. His family opposed his interest in art and he was forced to study at evening classes. He later worked as a labourer for the Paris Municipality: 'working like a slave' three nights a week and painting during daytime. In 1861 he met Cézanne and Pissarro at the Académie Suisse. In 1868 Guillaumin and Pissarro painted window blinds together. Guillaumin later worked as a labourer again. Pissarro wrote: 'Guillaumin ... works on his painting in the daytime and at his ditch-digging in the evening, what courage!'

Though poor (poverty prevented him joining the 1876 and 1879 exhibitions), Guillaumin contributed to every other Impressionist exhibition. He also encouraged new painters, including Paul Signac and Georges Seurat. In 1891 fortune smiled on Armand Guillaumin: he won a lottery prize of 100,000 francs and devoted himself to art. He died in June 1927, aged 86.

Maurice Brazil Prendergast 1859–1924

- Born 10 October 1859 in St Johns, Newfoundland, Canada.
- Died 1 February 1924 in New York City, USA.

Key works
Umbrellas in the Rain, 1899
May Day 1903, Central Park, 1903
Neponset Bay, 1914
Salem Park, Massachusetts, 1918

Maurice Brazil Prendergast was born into a humble family in St Johns, Newfoundland, Canada, in 1859. He had a twin sister, who died when he was seventeen, and a younger brother Charles. Little is known of his early life.

In 1868, the Prendergasts emigrated from Canada to Boston, in the USA. Maurice entered an American school, where he studied technical drawing. He left school at fourteen and took a job in a 'dry goods' store, selling haberdashery and textiles. He continued to study art at evening school. He often visited the Museum of Fine Arts in Boston and according to his brother, Charles, also sketched the countryside around Boston.

▌▌▌ *Prendergast is a painter of both townscapes and country scenes, and is best known for pictures of people enjoying innocent pleasures and pursuits.*

By 1891 Maurice and Charles – also an artist – had saved enough money to travel to Europe. They crossed the Atlantic on a cattle boat, which was exporting live cattle to Europe. Maurice stayed in France for over three years, enrolling at the Académie Julien in Paris in 1891. He also studied at the Académie Colarossi.

Prendergast returned to Boston in 1894 and joined Charles in Winchester, Massachusetts. His art focused on people enjoying their leisure time, walking in the park or on the beach. His first gallery showing was at the Boston Art Club in 1895, and his first one-man show was at the Macbeth Gallery, New York, in 1900. He also spent several years travelling in Europe.

Despite the relative popularity of Impressionism in the USA, Prendergast found it difficult to establish himself. He and Charles were close and, for both artistic and economic reasons, shared studio space. Charles owned a successful picture framing business and supported his brother financially.

Prendergast exhibited widely and frequently, and by 1910 had evolved his own Post-Impressionist style. In 1908 he joined 'The Eight', a group of artists who broke with traditional styles then popular in America, who wanted to show 'real life' by means of quickly executed drawings, sketches and paintings, and who wished to develop an authentic American school of painting. The Eight exhibited only once, in 1908 at the Macbeth Gallery. Prendergast took part in this show but none of his paintings were sold. The Eight went on to form the nucleus of 'The Ash Can School', who painted the growing slums, their poverty-stricken residents and the increasing number of social 'outcasts' in the USA.

In 1923, gravely ill in a New York City hospital and shortly before his death, Prendergast won a $1000 prize and bronze medal from the Corcoran Gallery in Washington, DC. He is reported to have said: 'I'm glad they've found out I'm not crazy, anyway.' He died in February 1924.

Neponset Bay, by Maurice Brazil Prendergast (1914)
Prendergast helped organise the famous 1913 Armory Show at which he also exhibited. Respected by his avant-garde peers and discerning collectors and dealers, if not the American public, Prendergast was elected president of the Association of American Painters and Sculptors in 1914.

Pierre-Auguste Renoir 1841–1919

- Born 25 February 1841, Limoges, France.
- Died 3 December 1919, Cagnes-sur-Mer, France.

Key works

Lise with a Parasol, 1867
La Grenouillère, 1869
Le Bal au Moulin de la Galette, 1876
Mme Charpentier and Her Children, 1878
Le Déjeuner des Canotiers, 1881
Young Girls at the Piano, 1892

Pierre-Auguste Renoir was born in Limoges, the fifth son of a tailor and a dressmaker. The family moved to Paris in 1846 and Renoir was educated at a free Catholic school run by the Christian Brothers. He showed promise as a musician and sang in the parish choir. At the age of thirteen, having shown early artistic talent, Auguste was apprenticed to a firm of porcelain painters, Lévy Frères et Compagnie. He decorated pieces with painted designs in their factory near the Louvre Museum in Paris. When he had free time, he visited the Louvre. He also took drawing lessons from a sculptor called Callouette.

Renoir developed a reputation as a painter of porcelain crockery. He began to decorate fans – used by society ladies to cool themselves – with fashionable scenes. He also painted shop blinds and even religious scenes on translucent material, in imitation of stained-glass windows, for the mobile tent-churches of missionaries. He was able to save a considerable amount of money and, in 1860, enrolled at the Gleyre **atelier**. Here he met Monet, Bazille and Sisley. Gleyre encouraged Renoir to copy at the Louvre. Renoir also enrolled for evening classes at the École des Beaux-Arts.

Without a wealthy family behind him, Renoir had to submit work to the **Salon** to build his reputation and therefore sell canvases. He exhibited at the Salon for the first time in 1864. (He later destroyed the painting, called *La Esmerelda*.) During the summer, Renoir painted **en plein air** with Bazille, Monet and Sisley in Fontainebleau Forest. In 1865 the Salon accepted two of his works. However, the 1865 jury was criticized by Salon members for its tolerance towards artists like Renoir. The 'realist' influence on Renoir's work did not please them and a new, hard-line jury rejected his submissions in 1866 and 1867. It was a bitter blow.

Renoir continued to live in precarious circumstances. He often relied on the generosity of friends, especially Bazille. He regularly visited the Café Guerbois, where he met Degas, Manet and the writer Émile Zola. He continued to submit pieces to the Salon, with increasing success. His painting of Lise Tréhot – *Lise with a Parasol* – was accepted by the Salon and greeted with acclaim by some critics. However, others accused him of emulating Manet.

Pierre-Auguste Renoir, by Jean-Frédéric Bazille (1867)
Poorer and coming from a more humble background than many of his peers, Renoir was much clearer about his need to sell paintings and make himself commercial if he was to make a successful living as an artist.

In 1869 Renoir and Monet painted together at the restaurant and bathing place, La Grenouillère. It was the stylistic breakthrough in the development of Impressionism.

During the **Franco-Prussian war**, Renoir joined the army. Posted to Bordeaux, he contracted dysentery. He returned to Paris in April 1871. He was deeply attached to this city – it was a place of animation, colour and excitement where he could secure portrait commissions and meet collectors. Renoir showed seven works at the 1874 Impressionist Exhibition. He exhibited again in 1876, 1877 and 1882. He continued to submit works to the **Salon** (to the annoyance of Degas, who thought it the worst kind of betrayal of Impressionist ideals). But the Salon was too important to Renoir: 'I'm not going to waste my time bearing a grudge against the Salon.'

Renoir's greatest success came at the 1879 Salon when a large group portrait, *Mme Charpentier and Her Children*, was accepted. He did not participate in the 1879 Impressionist Exhibition, realizing that many more people would see his work at the Salon and that anything he showed with the Impressionists would be ridiculed simply because it was shown with this group of artists. However, he did hold a one-man show at the offices of *La Vie Moderne* – an arts magazine aimed at promoting the Impressionists. By 1879, Renoir was accepting more portrait commissions.

In 1881, Renoir visited Italy. He painted several views of Venice – confessing to the art dealer Durand-Ruel that most were finished in his Paris studio. In March 1882, Durand-Ruel took charge of the seventh Impressionist Exhibition, hoping to restore the unity of the group. Renoir exhibited 26 pieces – including *Le Déjeuner des Canotiers* – which were warmly received.

On the way back from Italy, Renoir had visited Cézanne in L'Estaque, in the South of France. Impressed by Cézanne's work and influenced by classical pieces he had seen in Italy, Renoir told Durand-Ruel he had 'reached the end of Impressionism'. He began to develop a harder, carefully structured and more classical style of painting. *The Bathers* (1887) typified this change. Pissarro commented: 'I do not understand what he is trying to do.' However, many liked it: 'I think,' Renoir wrote to Durand-Ruel, 'I have advanced ... in the public approval.' Commercial pressure forced him to change back to his previous style after three years. Durand-Ruel had spent a lot of time persuading buyers to appreciate Renoir's work and thought they would be reluctant to accept a change.

There were also changes in Renoir's personal situation. In 1885, Aline Charigot bore him a son, Pierre. Of humble birth, Charigot had come to Paris to be a seamstress. Renoir met her in 1880 and used her as a model – notably in *Le Déjeuner des Canotiers*. When she and Renoir married in 1890, five years after Pierre's birth, it was the first that many of Renoir's friends knew of the relationship! Aline bore him two more sons: Jean (born 1894) and Claude – 'Coco' – (born 1901). During the 1880s and 90s, the family lived in the grandly named 'Château des Brouillards' – a ramshackle collection of buildings in a seedy part of Montmartre in Paris.

La Grenouillère, by Auguste Renoir (1869)
Though Renoir and Monet painted the same scene, Renoir placed greater emphasis on the islet and the people on it, indicating the preference he would always show for the human subject.

Despite the fact that Renoir created some of the most memorable images of women, his attitudes to women were less complementary. Similarly, his paintings portrayed working people with great dignity but his opinions about them were reactionary. 'Education,' he once said to Morisot's daughter Julie Manet, 'is the downfall of the working classes.'

In 1888, Renoir suffered his first attack of neuralgia, an illness of the nervous system, which temporarily paralysed his face. Four years later, in 1892, France honoured Renoir, buying his *Girls at the Piano* (1892). There was a major **retrospective** at Durand-Ruel's gallery. In 1894, Aline's cousin Gabrielle Renard joined the Renoirs to look after their son Jean. She stayed for twenty years and became Renoir's model. Many of his paintings were now a family record, and Renoir often returned to the theme of the mother and child.

■■ *Le Déjeuner des Canotiers (The Luncheon of the Boating Party),* by Auguste Renoir (1881)
In 1881, Renoir completed this painting that would become one of his most famous works. It features, amongst others, Renoir's future wife, Aline Charigot (on the left, holding a dog), and the artist Gustave Caillebotte (sitting on the right).

In 1896, after the death of Berthe Morisot, Renoir and his family took care of her daughter, Julie Manet. Renoir began to suffer from rheumatoid arthritis, a crippling disease of the joints. In time it would almost completely disable him – though he never let it stop him painting. The family spent more time in Cagnes-sur-Mer, in the South of France. In 1900, Renoir was made a *Chevalier de la Légion d'Honneur* and was later promoted to *Officier* and *Commandant*. He was also celebrated enough to have his work faked by unscrupulous artists and dealers! In 1907, Renoir bought land in Cagnes-sur-Mer and had a house built there.

By 1908, Renoir's work was being shown all around the world, including New York and Venice. He remained approachable and enthusiastic. When questioned by an American painter, he said: 'I have no rules and no methods; anyone can look at my materials or watch how I paint.' Now unable to walk, Renoir was carried to his studio and painted from a wheelchair, the paintbrushes tied into his crippled hands with ribbons.

Renoir became popular in Germany and was a major influence on the Expressionists. By 1913, he had exhibited in Munich, Berlin, Dresden and Stuttgart. To compensate for failing eyesight, he began to experiment with sculpture and, in 1913, employed a 23-year-old sculptor, Richard Guino, as both teacher and assistant. The years of World War I (1914–18) were hard for Renoir. In October 1914, both his sons Jean and Pierre were wounded in action. In June 1915, Aline died, age 56, of a heart attack after visiting Jean in hospital.

Renoir was now the most celebrated artist in France. When one of his paintings was hung in the National Gallery, London, in 1917, artists and critics sent him a testimonial: 'From the moment your picture was hung ... we had the joy of recognizing that one of our contemporaries had taken ... his place among the great masters of the European tradition.' Renoir survived into the first year of peace, and died of pneumonia at home in Cagnes-sur-Mer, on 3 December 1919, aged 78.

Alfred Sisley 1839–99

- Born 30 October 1839, Paris.
- Died 29 January 1899, Moret–sur–Loing, France.

Key works

Snow at Louveciennes, 1874
Foggy Morning, Voisins, 1874
Floods at Port-Marly, 1876
Beside the Loing, Saint-Mammes, 1885

Alfred Sisley, by Pierre-Auguste Renoir (1864)
After meeting at the Gleyre Atelier, Monet's influence was particularly strong and Sisley devoted himself to landscape painting.

Alfred Sisley was born in Paris to wealthy English parents. His father Guillaume ran a successful import-export business between France and South America dealing in artificial flowers, silks, feathers and gloves. His mother was called Felicia Sell. Alfred enjoyed a privileged, essentially French upbringing with his brother, Henri, and two sisters, Aline and Emily.

In 1857, as an eighteen-year-old, Sisley was sent by his family to study commerce in London. He spent most of his time in museums and art galleries. It seems likely Sisley was influenced by the Pre-Raphaelites – artists working in London who believed that art should be faithful to nature. However, no examples of work he completed in London exist today.

By the time he returned to Paris in 1862 Sisley knew he wanted to study art. In contrast to many of his peers, Sisley had a father who encouraged his son's artistic ambitions and, with a generous allowance, Sisley enrolled at the Gleyre **atelier**, where he met Monet, Renoir and Bazille. He also travelled widely, and painted extensively in England and Wales.

Sisley's early life was happy and free of worry, thanks to his allowance. Renoir called Sisley 'a delightful human being'. According to the accepted details of his life, Sisley married Marie-Eugénie Lescouezec, a model and florist who came from Toul, in the Lorraine region of France. Little is known about her. Renoir wrote that she had taken up modelling because 'her family had been ruined in some financial venture'. Evidence suggests the couple never married. They had two children, Pierre (born 1867) and Jeanne (born 1869). Sisley and Marie-Eugénie remained devoted to each other for the rest of their lives.

The 1860s were a good time for Sisley. He began to submit work to the **Salon** and the first acceptance was in 1866. The **Franco–Prussian War** in 1870 was a turning point in Sisley's life. It is thought he stayed in France during the war but there is evidence that some of his family – and possibly Sisley himself – did spend some time in London. As a consequence of the War, the family business collapsed. The shock affected the health of Sisley's father and he died in 1871. Sisley and his young family were now entirely dependent financially on his art. He became more prolific in his output, but suffered profound financial hardship. In 1879 he was even evicted for non-payment of rent. Helped by a wealthy publisher, the Sisleys settled in Moret-sur-Loing in 1880. In the 1880s, Sisley's work was shown to the art dealer Durand-Ruel, but even he could not sell it. In 1897, a major **retrospective** was largely ignored.

In old age Sisley avoided his former comrades. Asked to name his favourite artists, he pointedly ignored the names of his contemporaries. In October 1898, Marie-Eugénie died, having been nursed devotedly through her illness by her husband. Soon after, Alfred realized his own end was near and summoned his old friend, Monet, who rushed to be with him. Sisley died in January 1899 of cancer of the throat.

▮▮▮ *Flood at Port-Marly,* by Alfred Sisley (1876)
One of several paintings Sisley completed showing the effects of flooding on towns and villages in France.

The Next Generation

It is almost impossible to overestimate the influence of the Impressionists and their importance for the generation of artists who followed them. Camille Pissarro personally advised and inspired a new generation of artists: Paul Gauguin, Paul Signac, Georges Seurat, Paul Cézanne, Vincent van Gogh.

Neo-Impressionism and Pointillism

Neo-Impressionism was both a development of Impressionism and a reaction to it. While the Impressionists sought to be realistic, the Neo-Impressionists claimed that their work was more scientific. Neo-Impressionists like Signac, Seurat and, for a while, Pissarro, applied a scientific understanding of colour to Impressionism to create what they termed **Pointillism** – dots of colour which when viewed from a distance achieved an intense brightness. They earned the name **Neo-Impressionists** when they showed works at the final Impressionist exhibition in 1886.

Georges Seurat

George Seurat was born in Paris in 1859. He entered the École des Beaux-Arts in 1878 to study art. He was interested in science and particularly in the way the human eye sees colour. His studies led him to develop the theory of Pointillism.

In 1884, Seurat joined the **Salon des Indépendants**. Though Seurat chose common Impressionist subjects, such as landscapes and popular entertainment, he adopted traditional techniques of preparation and execution. He also departed from Impressionist ideas when, instead of trying to record scenes objectively, he attempted to express his own emotional responses to those scenes.

Post-Impressionism

The **Post-Impressionists** were artists who had moved on from or had been directly influenced by Impressionism – in particular Cézanne, Gauguin and van Gogh. The name Post-Impressionism was first used by an English art critic called Roger Fry to describe art from the period around 1880 to 1905.

Other influences

Pissarro also advised Matisse, who moved from imitating the Impressionists to **Fauvism**. Pissarro also encouraged the young Francis Picabia who moved from **Cubism** to **Dadaism** and **Surrealism**. Pablo Picasso, who was arguably the most influential artist of the modern age, had long been inspired by the Impressionists, especially Renoir and Degas.

Vincent van Gogh

Vincent van Gogh grew up in the small town of Groot Zundert in the Netherlands. At sixteen, he was employed at an art gallery run by his uncle and in 1873, he was sent to work in the London branch of the firm.

In 1881 he returned to Holland to paint. He sold nothing and was supported financially by his brother Theo. In 1885, he left for Paris where Theo was now working. He encountered the work of the Impressionists and met, among others, Pissarro, Gauguin and Seurat.

Influenced by Impressionism and by Japanese art, van Gogh began to express his own responses to what he saw rather than simply reproduce it. He travelled to Arles, in the South of France, in 1888. Between increasingly frequent bouts of depression and nervous illness, he produced an incredible number of canvases. After a violent argument with Gauguin, van Gogh famously cut off his own ear. Gauguin left, and van Gogh was hospitalized in the nearby asylum, where he continued to paint frantically.

The influence of the Impressionists was enormous. Virtually every movement in modern art grew from Impressionism. It changed the way both artists and non-artists see the world around them. Today, the numbers of people visiting Impressionist exhibitions and the incredible prices paid for works by Impressionist painters show how popular it remains.

■■ *The Church at Auvers,*
by Vincent van Gogh (1890)
In 1886, after Camille Pissarro met Vincent van Gogh for the first time, he warned that van Gogh 'would either go mad or leave the Impressionists far behind'. Until this point, van Gogh's work had been dark and gloomy. After Pissarro explained his own technique and theory of colour, van Gogh began to experiment – to immediate and dramatic effect.

Timeline

1830   Camille Pissarro born

1832   Édouard Manet born

1834   Edgar Degas born

1839   Alfred Sisley and Paul Cézanne born

1840   Claude Monet born

1841   Berthe Morisot, Pierre–Auguste Renoir and Frédéric Bazille born

1844   Mary Cassatt born

1848   Revolution in France; Gustave Caillebotte born

1850   Manet enters the **atelier** of Thomas Couture

1859   Childe Hassam and Maurice Brazil Prendergast born; Monet studies at the Académie Suisse in Paris; Pissarro exhibits a small landscape at the **Salon**; Bazille starts medical studies in Montpellier

1860   Renoir enrols at the atelier of Charles Gleyre

1861   The Salon accepts Manet's *The Spanish Guitar Player*; Cézanne arrives in Paris

1862   Morisot takes lessons with the artist Corot; Monet and Bazille join the atelier of Charles Gleyre

1863   Manet marries Suzanne Leenhoff; the Salon rejects *Le Déjeuner sur L'Herbe*; **Salon des Refusés** set up

1864   Morisot has work accepted by the Salon; Renoir accepted at the Salon

1865	Salon accepts Manet's *Olympia*; Monet shows two seascapes
1866	*Camille: Woman in the Green Dress* by Monet acclaimed at the Salon; Alfred Sisley marries Eugénie Lesconezec
1870	Declaration of the **Franco-Prussian War**
1871	Pissarro marries Julie Vellay in London before returning to France
1874	First Impressionist Exhibition; Morisot marries Eugène Monet; Cassatt enrols at the atelier of Charles Chaplin
1876	Second Impressionist Exhibition
1877	Third Impressionist Exhibition
1879	Fourth Impressionist Exhibition
1880	Fifth Impressionist Exhibition
1881	Sixth Impressionist Exhibition; Manet made a *Chevalier de la Légion d'Honneur*
1882	Seventh Impressionist Exhibition
1886	Eighth (and last) Impressionist Exhibition
1889	Fund established to buy Manet's *Olympia* for the French nation
1890	Renoir marries Aline Charigot
1900	Renoir made a *Chevalier de la Légion d'Honneur*
1914	Outbreak of World War I

Glossary

anti-Semitic person who hates or acts against people because they are Jewish

art establishment the establishment believed in idealization in art, of both people and places. They tended to reject art that did not fall within their strict definitions.

atelier art school run by a well-known painter. The best-known atelier was run by Charles Gleyre, where Bazille, Renoir, Monet and Sisley met.

baccalaureate French school qualification

cataracts gradual misting up of the lens of the eye, causing progressive loss of vision

classical describes art that follows formal rules of construction and idealization rather than individual expression or truth

Cubism art movement of the early 20th century that abandoned notions of perspective and was recognized as one of the major turning points in western art. Though influenced by Cézanne, the artists most closely associated with Cubism are Georges Braque and Pablo Picasso.

Dadaism violent, provocative and anarchic art that mirrored the disillusionment many young artists felt with World War I

draughtsmanship the technical ability to draw well

Dreyfus Affair named after Alfred Dreyfus (1859–1935), a Jewish officer in the French army, who was wrongfully jailed for passing military secrets to the Germans. A campaign was started to have him freed and 'The Dreyfus Affair', as it became known, divided France. He was eventually found not guilty in 1906.

en plein air painting in the open air so as to see colours in their true light

Expressionism art in which traditional ideas are abandoned in favour of a style which exaggerates feelings or expressions. Van Gogh, an important forerunner of Expressionism, exaggerated nature 'to express ... man's terrible passions'. Expressionist groups emerged in France – the Fauvists – and in Germany in the first decade of the 20th century.

Fauvism Expressionist style of painting inspired by the Neo-Impressionists and Cézanne, based on intense and vivid non-naturalistic colours. It emerged as the first major avant–garde development in the 20th century. The leading lights were Henri Matisse and Paul Signac.

Franco-Prussian War (1870–1) war between Prussia and France that inflicted crushing defeats on France at Sedan, Metz and the Siege of Paris, and resulted in a humiliating peace at the Treaty of Frankfurt

Inquisition Catholic organization established during the 13th century, and surviving until the 19th century in Spain, designed to counter the threat of Christian heretics and non-believers to the supremacy of the Roman Catholic Church

motif   dominant or distinctive figure or subject in an artistic composition

Neo-Impressionism   term used to describe a movement that grew out of Impressionism, fundamentally concerned with light and colour but one based on scientific principles. Seurat, Signac and Pissarro were its best-known artists.

Old Masters   collective term for paintings completed by the great names of artistic history

palette   choice of colours of a particular artist or the actual board that an artist mixes his paints on while painting

Paris Commune   defeat by Prussia left many unhappy with the government and the incompetent, often treacherous way it had defended them. In March 1871, Parisian Republicans seized the city. French troops entered Paris on 21 May. For a week great bloodshed ensued. The last of the Communards were cornered and massacred, leaving a bitter legacy.

perspective   method of representing space and depth on a flat surface

Pointillism   technique of using small dots of colour so that when viewed from a distance a bright and vibrant colour mix is achieved. Associated with the Neo-Impressionists.

Post-Impressionism   term applied to the various trends in art that developed from or in reaction to Impressionism. Names include Cézanne, Gauguin, Seurat, Signac and van Gogh.

retrospective   a look back at an artist's career, to show the development of their work over time

Salon   annual exhibition of the French Royal Academy of Painting and Sculpture

Salon des Indépendants   exhibitions started in 1884 by Seurat and Signac in opposition to the official Salon

Salon des Refusés   exhibition ordered by Emperor Napoleon III and held in Paris in 1863 showing work that had been refused by the official Salon. Manet's *Déjeuner sur l'Herbe* was the centrepiece.

Siege of Paris   see Franco-Prussian War

Surrealism   art movement originating in France in the 1920s and characterized by the bizarre, dreamlike, irrational and absurd

Symbolism   art movement founded in reaction to Impressionism that aimed to express mystical and spiritual aspects of life in a visual medium. It often explored both religious and erotic images and concepts.

syphilis   serious sexually transmitted disease that can go into remission for many years before re-infecting the sufferer in a variety of different ways

Resources

List of famous works

Jean-Frédéric Bazille (1841–70)
Monet after his Accident at the Inn in Chailly, 1865, Musée d'Orsay, Paris
The Artist's Family on a Terrace near Montpellier, 1867–8, Musée d'Orsay, Paris
View of the Village, 1868, Musée Fabre, Montpellier
Summer Scene, Bathers, 1869, Fogg Art Museum, Cambridge, USA
Studio in the Rue de la Condamine, 1870, Musée d'Orsay, Paris

Gustave Caillebotte (1848–94)
Les Raboteurs de Parquet (The Floor Scrapers), 1875, Musée d'Orsay, Paris
Pont de l'Europe, 1876, Musée du Petit Palais, Geneva
Street in Paris, A Rainy Day, 1877, The Art Institute of Chicago
Self-Portrait, 1892, Musée d'Orsay, Paris

Mary Cassatt (1844–1926)
Woman and Child Driving, 1879, Philadelphia Museum of Art
Mother about to Wash her Sleepy Child, 1880, Los Angeles County Museum of Art
Lydia Crocheting in the Garden at Marly, 1880, Musée d'Orsay, Paris
A Woman in Black at the Opera, 1880, Museum of Fine Arts, Boston
The Loge, 1882, National Gallery of Art, Washington DC
Children Playing on the Beach, 1884, National Gallery of Canada

Paul Cézanne (1839–1906)
Dr Gachet's House at Auvers, 1873, Musée d'Orsay, Paris
House of the Hanged Man, 1873, Musée d'Orsay, Paris
The Bathers, 1875–6
Portrait of Victor Chocquet, 1875–7, Private collection
The Seine at Bercy, 1876–8
Madame Cézanne in a Red Armchair, 1877,
Still Life with Compotier, 1879–80, Private collection
L'Estaque, 1885, Private collection
Large Bathers, 1895, Barnes Foundation, Merion
Quarry and Mont Sainte-Victoire, 1898–1900, Philadelphia Museum of Art

Edgar Degas (1834–1917)
The Bellelli Family, 1860–2, Musée d'Orsay, Paris
Carriage at the Races, 1869, Museum of Fine Arts, Boston
Woman Ironing, 1869, Neue Pinakothek, Munich
The Orchestra of the Opéra, 1870, Musée d'Orsay, Paris
The Cotton Exchange in New Orleans, 1873, Fogg Art Museum, Cambridge, USA
Ballet Rehearsal, 1873–4, Musée d'Orsay, Paris
The Dance Class, 1873–4, Musée d'Orsay, Paris
L'Absinthe, 1875–6, Musée d'Orsay, Paris
The Star, 1876–7, Musée d'Orsay, Paris
Miss La La at the Cirque Fernando, 1879, National Gallery, London
At the Milliners, 1882, Metropolitan Museum of Art, New York
Ballet Scene, 1907, National Gallery of Art, Washington DC

Childe Hassam (1859–1935)
Rainy Day, Columbus Avenue, Boston, 1885, Toledo Museum of Art, Toledo, USA
July 14 Rue Daunon, 1910, Metropolitan Museum of Art, New York
Manhattan's Misty Sunset, 1911, Butler Institute of American Art, Ohio
Fifth Avenue, April Morning 1917, 1917, Sheldon Memorial Art Gallery, Nebraska
Church at Gloucester, 1918, Metropolitan Museum of Art, New York

Édouard Manet (1832–83)
The Spanish Guitar Player, 1861, Metropolitan Museum of Art, New York
Le Déjeuner sur L'Herbe, 1863, Musée d'Orsay, Paris
Olympia, 1863, Musée d'Orsay, Paris
The Execution of Emperor Maximilian, 1868–9, Städtische Kunsthalle, Mannheim
The Balcony, 1868–9, Musée d'Orsay, Paris
Le Bon Bock, 1873, Philadelphia Museum of Art
Repose: Portrait of Berthe Morisot, 1869–70, Rhode Island School of Design, Museum of Art, Providence
Nana, 1877, Hamburger Kunsthalle, Hamburg
Bar at the Folies-Bergère, 1881–2, Courtauld Institute, London

Claude Monet (1840–1926)
Déjeuner sur l'Herbe, 1865, Pushkin Museum, Moscow
La Terrasse à Sainte-Adresse, 1866, Metropolitan Museum of Art, New York
Camille: Woman in the Green Dress, 1866, Kunsthalle, Bremen
Women in the Garden, 1866–7, Musée d'Orsay, Paris
The Cradle – Camille with the Artist's Son, Jean, 1867, Musée d'Orsay, Paris
The Thames and the Houses of Parliament, 1871, National Gallery, London
Impression: Sunrise, 1872–3, Musée Marmottan, Paris
*Haystacks (series)*1890–1, Art Institute of Chicago and Metropolitan Museum
of Art, New York
Poplar Trees on the Epte River, 1891, Metropolitan Museum of Art, New York
The West Front of Rouen Cathedral (series), 1892, examples in Metropolitan
Museum of Art, New York, Museum Folkwang, Essen, Musée d'Orsay, Paris and
National Museum of Wales, Cardiff
Monet's Garden. The Irises, 1900, Musée d'Orsay, Paris
The Nymphéas (Waterlilies), 1916–26, Orangerie, Musée National du
Louvre, Paris

Berthe Morisot (1841–95)
The Mother and Sister of the Artist, 1870, National Gallery of Art,
Washington DC
The Cradle, 1872, Musée d'Orsay, Paris
Hide and Seek, 1873, Private collection
Young Woman in a Ball Gown, 1876, Musée d'Orsay, Paris
Summer, 1878, Musée Fabre, Montpellier
Eugène Manet and his Daughter at Bourgival, 1881, Private collection

Camille Pissarro (1830–1903)
Lower Norwood, London: Snow Effect, 1870, National Gallery, London
Lordship Lane Station, Dulwich, 1871, Courtauld Institute, London
The Red Roofs: Corner of the Village, Winter Effect, 1877, Musée d'Orsay, Paris
Portrait of Félix Pissarro, 1881, Tate Modern, London
The Little Country Maid, 1882, Tate Modern, London
The Gleaners, 1889, Offentliche Kunstsammlung, Kunstmuseum, Basel
The Rooftops of Old Rouen, Grey Weather, 1896, Toledo Museum of Art,
Toledo, USA
The Place du Théâtre Français, 1898, Minneapolis Institute of Art

Maurice Brazil Prendergast (1859–1924)
Central Park, 1901, 1901, Whitney Museum of American Art, New York
The Promenade, 1913, Whitney Museum of American Art, New York
Neponset Bay, 1914, Sheldon Memorial Art Gallery, Nebraska
Salem Park, Massachusetts, 1918, Sheldon Memorial Art Gallery, Nebraska

Pierre-Auguste Renoir (1841–1919)
Lise with a Parasol, 1867, Museum Folkwang, Essen
La Grenouillère, 1869, National Museum, Stockholm
Le Bal au Moulin de la Galette, 1876, Musée d'Orsay, Paris
Mme Charpentier and Her Children, 1878, Metropolitan Museum of Art, New York
Le Déjeuner des Canotiers, 1881, Phillips Collection, Washington DC
Washerwomen, 1888, Baltimore Museum of Art
Young Girls at the Piano, 1892, Musée d'Orsay, Paris
Gabrielle and Jean, 1895, Musée de l'Orangerie, Paris

Alfred Sisley (1839–99)
The Square at Argentuil, 1872, Musée d'Orsay, Paris
Snow at Louveciennes, 1874, Courtauld Institute, London
Foggy Morning, Voisins, 1874, Musée d'Orsay, Paris
Floods at Port-Marly, 1876, Musée d'Orsay, Paris
Canal du Loing at Saint Mammes, 1885, Philadelphia Museum of Art

Where to see the Impressionists

France
Musée d'Orsay, Paris
A superb collection including work by Monet, Manet, Bazille, Cézanne, Caillebotte, Degas, Renoir, Sisley, Morisot and Pissarro.

Musée Marmottan, Paris
65 Monets, plus works by Morisot, Pissarro, Renoir, Sisley, Boudin, Signac, Manet.

There are also major Impressionist collections in Aix-en-Provence, Aix-Les-Bains, Cagnes-sur-Mer, Giverny, Le Havre, Montpellier and Pau.

United Kingdom
Courtauld Institute, London
Works by Monet, Manet, Cézanne, Degas, Renoir, Sisley and Pissarro.

National Gallery, London
Large Impressionist collection including work by Monet, Cézanne, Degas, Manet, Pissarro and Morisot.

Tate Modern, London
Several works by Degas, Monet, Pissarro, Sisley and Manet.

Other collections: Fitzwilliam Museum, Cambridge; Ashmolean Museum, Oxford; National Gallery of Scotland, Edinburgh; Burrell Collection, Glasgow; National Museum of Wales, Cardiff.

USA
Boston Museum of Fine Arts, Boston
One of the largest collections of Impressionist works in the USA – includes 40 works by Monet, 20 by Renoir, 15 Degas and works by Manet, Sisley, Cézanne, Caillebotte, Guillaumin, Morisot and Cassatt.

Art Institute of Chicago, Chicago
Works by Bazille, Caillebotte, Cassatt, Cézanne, Degas, Manet and Renoir.

Metropolitan Museum of Art, New York
Another splendid collection: works by Cassatt, Cézanne, Degas, Gauguin, Guillaumin, Manet, Monet, Morisot, Pissarro, Renoir and Sisley.

Museum of Modern Art, New York
Large collection including 22 Cézannes, plus pieces by Degas, Monet, Renoir.

National Gallery of Art, Washington DC
Outstanding collection of Impressionist art, including many Manets, and work by Cassatt, Degas, Cézanne, Morisot, Pissarro, Renoir, Bazille, Guillaumin and Sisley.

Other collections: Phillips Collection, Washington DC; Cleveland Museum of Art, Cleveland; Nelson-Atkins Museum of Art, Kansas City; Philadelphia Museum of Art, Philadelphia; Harvard University; Houston Museum of Fine Arts; Los Angeles County Museum.

Australia
National Gallery of Australia, Canberra

Useful websites
Most major museums now have websites and several run 'virtual galleries', which reproduce artworks, offer information about them and give biographical details about the artists.

Further reading

General

Impressionist Women, Edward Lucie-Smith, George Weidenfeld and Nicolson ltd, London, 1989

The History of Impressionism, John Rewald, 4th edition, Museum of Modern Art, New York, 1973; Secker and Warburg, London, 1973

Impressionist Dreams, John Russell Taylor, Barrie and Jenkins, London, 1990

The Impressionists, William Gaunt, Thames and Hudson, London, 1985

The Chronicle of Impressionism, Bernard Denvir, Thames and Hudson, London, 1993

Modern Art – Impressionism to Post-Modernism, edited by David Britt, Thames and Hudson, London, 1989

Impressionism, Mark Powell-Jones, Phaidon, London, 1994

The artists

Frédéric Bazille, Francois Daulte, Le Bibliothèque des Arts, Paris

Bazille, Dianne W Pitman, Penn State University Press, USA, 1998

Gustave Caillebotte, Kirk Varndoe, Yale University, New Haven/London, 1987

Mary Cassatt, Griselda Pollock, Thames and Hudson, London, 1998

Mary Cassatt: A Private World, Sara R Witzling, Universe Pubs. New York, 1991

Mary Cassatt, Debra N Mancoff, Stewart, Tabori and Chang, London, 1998

First Impressions: Mary Cassatt, Susan E Mayer, Harry N. Abrams, New York, 1990

Mary Cassatt: A Life, Nancy Mowll Mathews, Yale University, 1998

Cézanne, John Rewald, Harry N.Abrams, London/New York, 1986

Cézanne, Richard Verdi, Thames and Hudson, London, 1992

Degas, Keith Roberts, Phaidon Press, New York/London, 1992

Degas, Andrew Forge and Robert Gordon, Harry N.Abrams, New York/London, 1988

Childe Hassam: American Impressionist, Ulrich Hiesinger, Prestel USA, 1999

Eyewitness Art: Manet, Patricia Wright, Dorling Kindersley Publishing, London/New York, 1993

Manet, John Richardson, Phaidon Press, New York/London, 1992

Monet, John House, Phaidon Press, New York/London, 1992

Berthe Morisot, Kathleen Adler and Tamar Garb, Phaidon Press, New York/London, 1987

Growing up with the Impressionists: The Diary of Julie Manet, Julie Manet, Sotheby Parke Bernet Pubs, London, 1987

Pissarro and Pointoise, Richard R Brettell, Yale University, New Haven/London, 1990

Pissarro, Christopher Lloyd, Phaidon, London, 1992

Renoir: His Art, Life and Letters, Barbara Ehrlich White, Harry N. Abrams, New York, 1988

Renoir, My Father, Jean Renoir, New York Review of Books, New York, 2001

Alfred Sisley, Vivienne Couldrey, David and Charles, Newton Abbott, 1992

Sisley, Richard Shone, Phaidon Press New York/London, 1994

Index